Launch into Literacy
Book 1

Jane Medwell
Maureen Lewis

OXFORD
UNIVERSITY PRESS

Contents

UNIT 1 — Writing to inform

The human skeleton (a report)	4–5
Understanding information	6
Homonyms	6
Fiction and non-fiction	7
Understanding a chart	8
Sentences	9
Verbs in sentences	10
The verb 'to be'	11

Another report — 12–13

Commas in lists	14
Past and present tense verbs	15

Writing a report — 16–17

UNIT 2 — Writing to entertain

The Hodgeheg (a novel)	18–19
Character and settings	20
What happens next?	21
Nouns	22
Nouns for names	23
Describing characters	24
Describing settings	25

A story plot — 26–27

A story blurb	26
Events in order	27
Characters speaking	28
Writing down talk	29

Writing a story — 30–31

UNIT 3

Writing to express

Mark's Fingers (a poem)	32–33
Using words	34
Verbs	35
Using sounds	36
Where things are	37

Words in a list poem 38–39
| Similes | 38 |
| Antonyms | 39 |

More words	40
One and more than one	41
Commas in lists	42
Conjunctions	43

Writing a list poem 44–45

UNIT 4

Writing to instruct

How to make a spinner (instructions)	46–47
Comprehension	48
Abbreviations	48
Events in order	49
Linking words	50
Words of command	51
What does it mean?	52
Definitions	53

More instructions 54–55
| Adverbs | 55 |

| Exclamation marks | 56 |
| Diagrams | 57 |

Writing instructions 58–59

UNIT 5

Writing to recount

Postcards (a holiday account)	60–61
Informing others	62
Past and present	63
Forming the past tense	64
He, she, it, they	65
Me, myself, I	66
Time lines	67

Two types of letter 68–69

| Addresses | 70 |
| Questions and statements | 71 |

Writing a letter 72–73

UNIT·1

Writing to inform

In this unit you will study how **non-chronological** reports are written. Reports give us information. At the end of the unit you will write your own non-chronological report.

opening definition tells the subject of the report

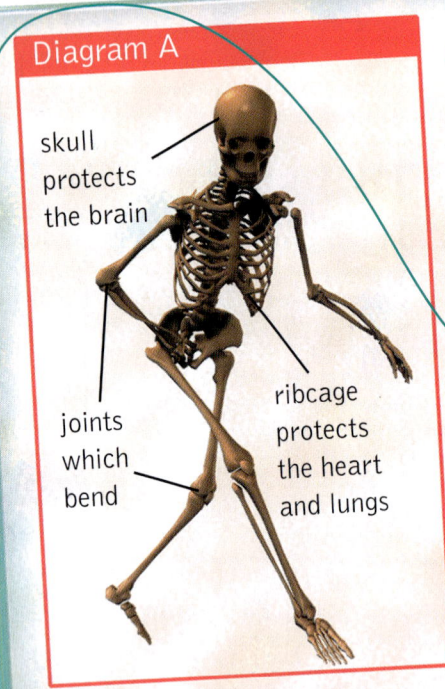

Diagram A

skull protects the brain

joints which bend

ribcage protects the heart and lungs

The human skeleton

The skeleton is the framework of the human body. It is a complicated structure of 206 bones and it has a number of important jobs. These are support, protection, movement and making new cells.

diagram

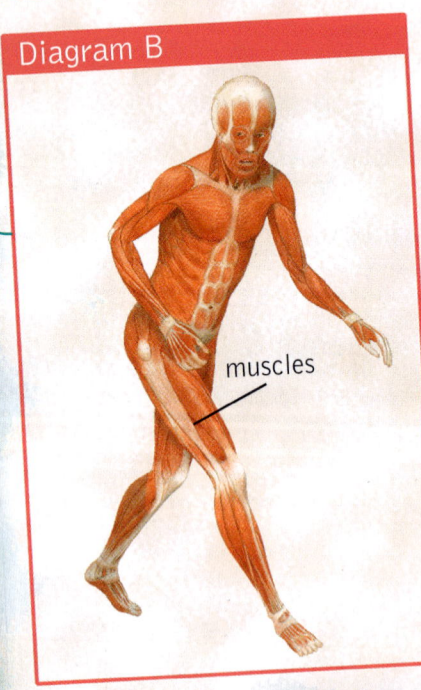

Diagram B

muscles

Support
The skeleton is a framework on which your muscles and skin hang. Diagram B shows how the muscles cover the human skeleton.

Protection
Important organs such as your heart, lungs, brain and kidneys are delicate. The bones of the skeleton protect these organs so that they do not get damaged. For example, the skull protects the brain and the ribs protect the heart and lungs.

28

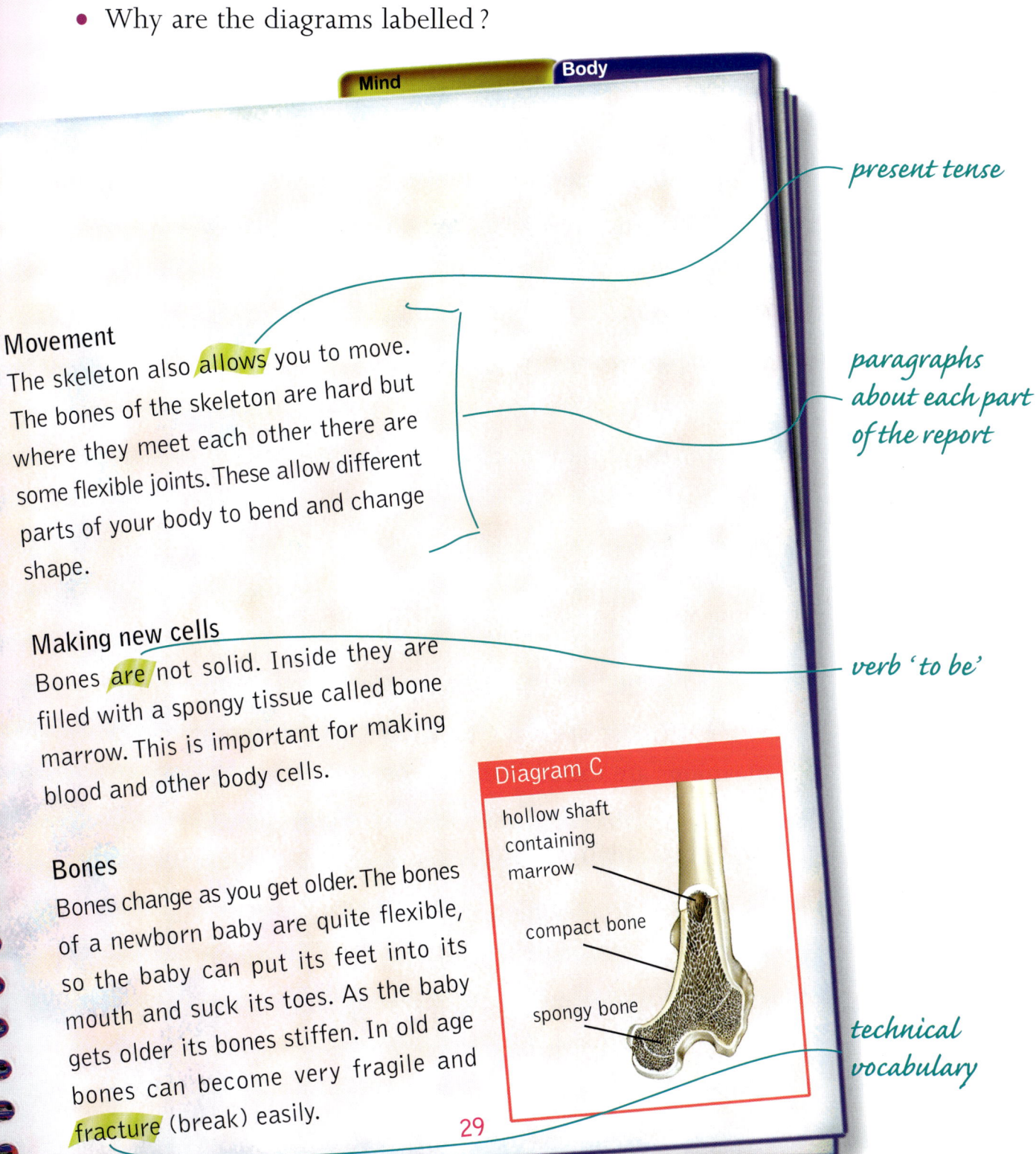

UNIT·1 **Writing to inform**

Text features: opening definition, non-chronological order, technical vocabulary, diagram

Look at how this explanation is written.
- What does the first sentence tell you?
- What are the headings in this report?
- Why does this passage include diagrams?
- Why are the diagrams labelled?

Mind   Body

— present tense

Movement
The skeleton also *allows* you to move. The bones of the skeleton are hard but where they meet each other there are some flexible joints. These allow different parts of your body to bend and change shape.

— paragraphs about each part of the report

Making new cells
Bones *are* not solid. Inside they are filled with a spongy tissue called bone marrow. This is important for making blood and other body cells.

— verb 'to be'

Diagram C
- hollow shaft containing marrow
- compact bone
- spongy bone

Bones
Bones change as you get older. The bones of a newborn baby are quite flexible, so the baby can put its feet into its mouth and suck its toes. As the baby gets older its bones stiffen. In old age bones can become very fragile and *fracture* (break) easily.

— technical vocabulary

29

5

UNIT·1 Writing to inform

Reading skills: comprehension, dictionary use
Words: technical words, homonyms

<u>Remember</u>
Use the information from the diagrams as well as information from the written report.

Understanding information

1 Reread the explanation about skeletons on pages 4 and 5.

2 Now answer these questions.
   a The frame of the human body is called
      the bones?   the skeleton?   the body?
   b Which part of the skeleton protects the heart?
   c List two types of bone.
   d List three reasons why we have a skeleton.

3 Answer these questions about some of the words in the passage.
   a Flexible means
      able to bend?   very large?   very small?
   b Fragile means
      tough?   very old?   easily broken?
   c Solid means
      without a space inside?   full up?   soft and spongy?

Homonyms

> Some words can have more than one meaning.
> EXAMPLE: cell – a place where prisoners are kept in prison.
>   cell – the smallest part of a living thing.
> Words that are spelt the same but have different meanings are called **homonyms**.

<u>Remember</u>
Use a dictionary to find the meanings of words you do not know.

1 Here are some more homonyms. Complete the **definitions**.

   a nail – a piece of metal used to fix materials together.   nail –

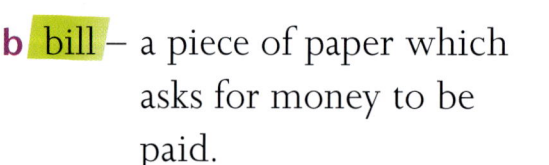

   b bill – a piece of paper which asks for money to be paid.   bill –

   c ear – the top part of a stalk of wheat or other grain.   ear –

Glossary
definition

6

Fiction and non-fiction

UNIT·1 Writing to inform

Text study: fiction/non-fiction
Vocabulary: technical words, labels

Here is a page from a story about skeletons called Funnybones.

1. How do you know the page from Funnybones is a fiction text? Give two reasons.

> A **fiction** book uses everyday words to name things.
> A **non-fiction** book uses more technical words.
> EXAMPLES: hip bone (fiction) pelvis (non-fiction)

2. Copy out and match up the everyday and technical words. The first one is done for you.

   back bones — pelvis
   hip bone — skull
   head bone — vertebrae

Remember
Use a dictionary to find the meanings of words you do not know.

> Fiction and non-fiction books contain different types of **illustration**. Fiction books often contain pictures. Non-fiction books often contain diagrams.

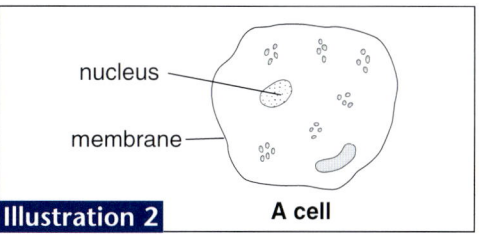

Illustration 1

Illustration 2 — A cell (nucleus, membrane)

3. Look at the illustrations above and answer these questions.
   a. Is Illustration 1 a picture or a diagram?
   b. Why does Illustration 2 have labels?
   c. Which illustration would you find in a fiction book?

7

UNIT·1 Writing to inform

Reading skills: reading from a chart, comprehension

Understanding a chart

Charts can show a lot of information. This chart compares humans with cars.

How the human machine compares with the car

	Car	Human
Fuel	petrol or diesel fuel	food
Load-carrying ability	1000 kg	20 kg
Speed	up to 160 km per hour (100 mph)	up to 25 km per hour (15 mph)
Maintenance	service required once a year – some parts (e.g. tyres) need replacing regularly	mostly self-repairing – health checks needed and sometimes medical attention
Lifespan (typical)	10 years	75 years

57

1 Study the chart and look up any difficult words in the dictionary. Answer these questions.
   a How long does a car usually last?
   b 'Self-repairing' means
      a mechanic does repairs? it repairs itself without help?
      it does not need repairs?
   c Car tyres need replacing regularly
      to make them fit better?   because they wear out?
      to change the colour?

2 Use the information in the chart to complete these comparisons.
   EXAMPLE: A car is faster than a human.
   a The _____ is stronger than the _____.
   b A _____ lasts longer than a _____.

8

Sentences

> A **sentence** is a piece of writing which makes sense on its own. A sentence starts with a **capital letter** and ends with a **full stop**, **question mark** or **exclamation mark**.

UNIT·1 Writing to inform
Grammar: *sentences*

1 Some of the groups of words below are sentences. Pick out three sentences. Write them out adding capital letters and full stops.
   a ten years
   b cars last for about ten years
   c humans live for about 75 years
   d long life
   e humans eat food

Remember
Add capital letters and full stops.

2 Sentences make sense. Rearrange these words to make sentences.
   a food eat humans
   b cars fuel petrol as use
   c human a faster than is a car

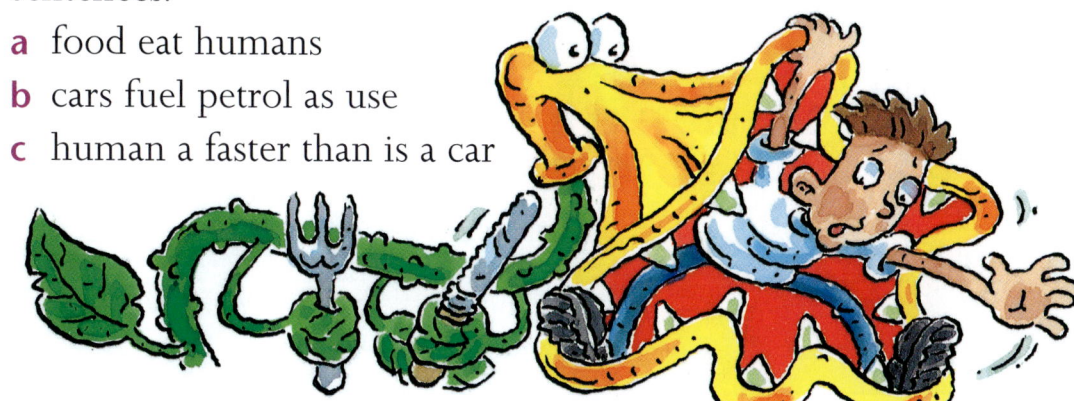

3 Write out these sentences, adding a word so that each sentence makes sense.

   a He fell over and ▢ his leg.
   b The old car ▢ along the road.
   c The children ▢ sweets in the playground.
   d Chris really ▢ happy.

Glossary
capital letter
full stop
question mark
exclamation mark

9

UNIT·1 Writing to inform

Grammar: *verbs*

Verbs in sentences

A **verb** is a word which tells us what people are doing or being.

EXAMPLE: Dad **fell** down the stairs.

Most **sentences** contain a verb.

Remember
Every sentence contains an idea, starts with a **capital letter** and ends with a **full stop**.

1 Look at these pictures from the book Funnybones.

2 Write out these sentences and put in verbs.
   a The skeletons ▇ the dog.
   b The dog ▇ at the skeletons.
   c The big skeleton ▇ a red hat.
   d The little skeleton ▇ the big skeleton.

3 We could use different verbs to say how the skeletons moved down the street. Put a different verb in each sentence. The first one has been done for you.
   a The skeletons *tiptoed* down the street.
   b The skeletons ▇ down the street.
   c The skeletons ▇ down the street.
   d The skeletons ▇ down the street.

Glossary
sentence
capital letter
full stop

The verb 'to be'

Some **sentences** in the report about skeletons on pages 4 and 5 use the **verb** 'is' and 'are'.

EXAMPLES: Bones **are** not solid.

The longest bone **is** the thigh bone.

'Is' and 'are' are part of a very important verb – the verb **'to be'**. The verb 'to be' changes if we are talking about one person (or thing) or more than one.

SINGULAR   PLURAL
I am   we are
you are   you are
he/she/it is they are

1 Write out these sentences with the correct version of the verb 'to be' in the spaces.

EXAMPLE: He is outside the house.

a She ___ with her friend.
b They ___ both good at sums.
c We ___ at Sally's house.
d The skeleton ___ the framework of the human body.
e Bones ___ strong.

2 This writer has muddled up the **singular** and **plural** of the verb 'to be'. Rewrite the explanation putting in the correct word for each highlighted word.

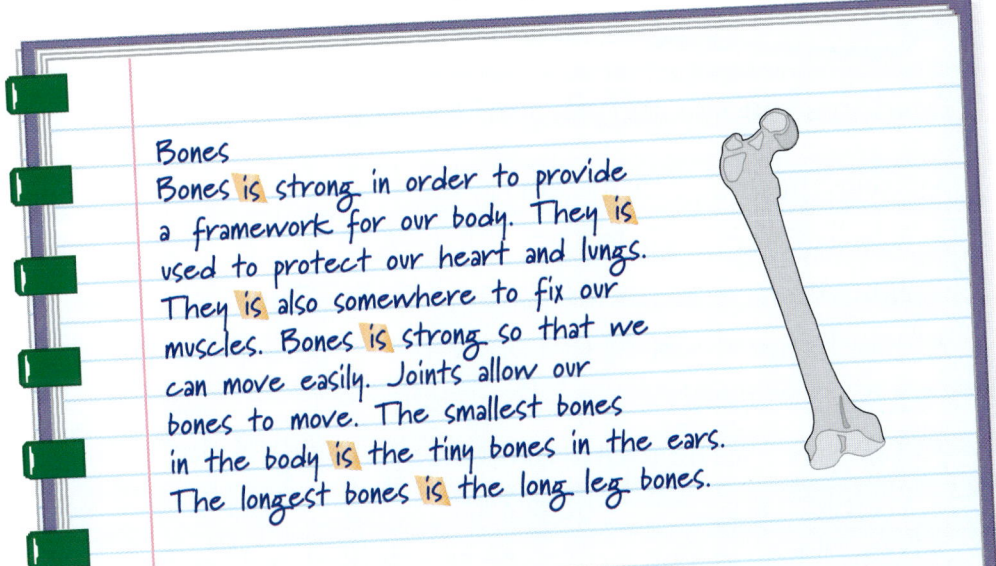

> Bones
> Bones **is** strong in order to provide a framework for our body. They **is** used to protect our heart and lungs. They **is** also somewhere to fix our muscles. Bones **is** strong so that we can move easily. Joints allow our bones to move. The smallest bones in the body **is** the tiny bones in the ears. The longest bones **is** the long leg bones.

UNIT·1 Writing to inform

Grammar: the verb 'to be'

Glossary

sentence
verb
singular
plural

11

Another report

Teeth

the subject of the report — Teeth are the part of the body used for biting, tearing and chewing food.

The outside part of the tooth is covered with a layer of enamel. This is the hardest material in the human body. Tooth enamel cannot be replaced if it is damaged or worn.

verb 'to be' — It is important to look after your teeth.

present tense — Teeth develop in the jawbone before birth. The first teeth (milk teeth) start to appear at about 6 months of age. They fall out at around 6 or 7 years of age and are replaced by adult teeth.

1 Read this report carefully and look at the diagram.

2 Answer these questions about teeth.
 a We use our teeth for
   hearing?   running?   biting and chewing?
 b The hardest part of the body is
   bone?   tooth enamel?   nails?
 c The part of the tooth you can see is called the
   root?   crown?   gum?
 d Why should you go to see the dentist regularly?

Glossary
verb
present tense

UNIT·1 Writing to inform

Reading skills: comprehension, reading a chart
Writing skills: completing a chart

Diagram A

A cross-section of a tooth

- crown
- enamel
- dentine
- pulp
- gum
- root

diagram

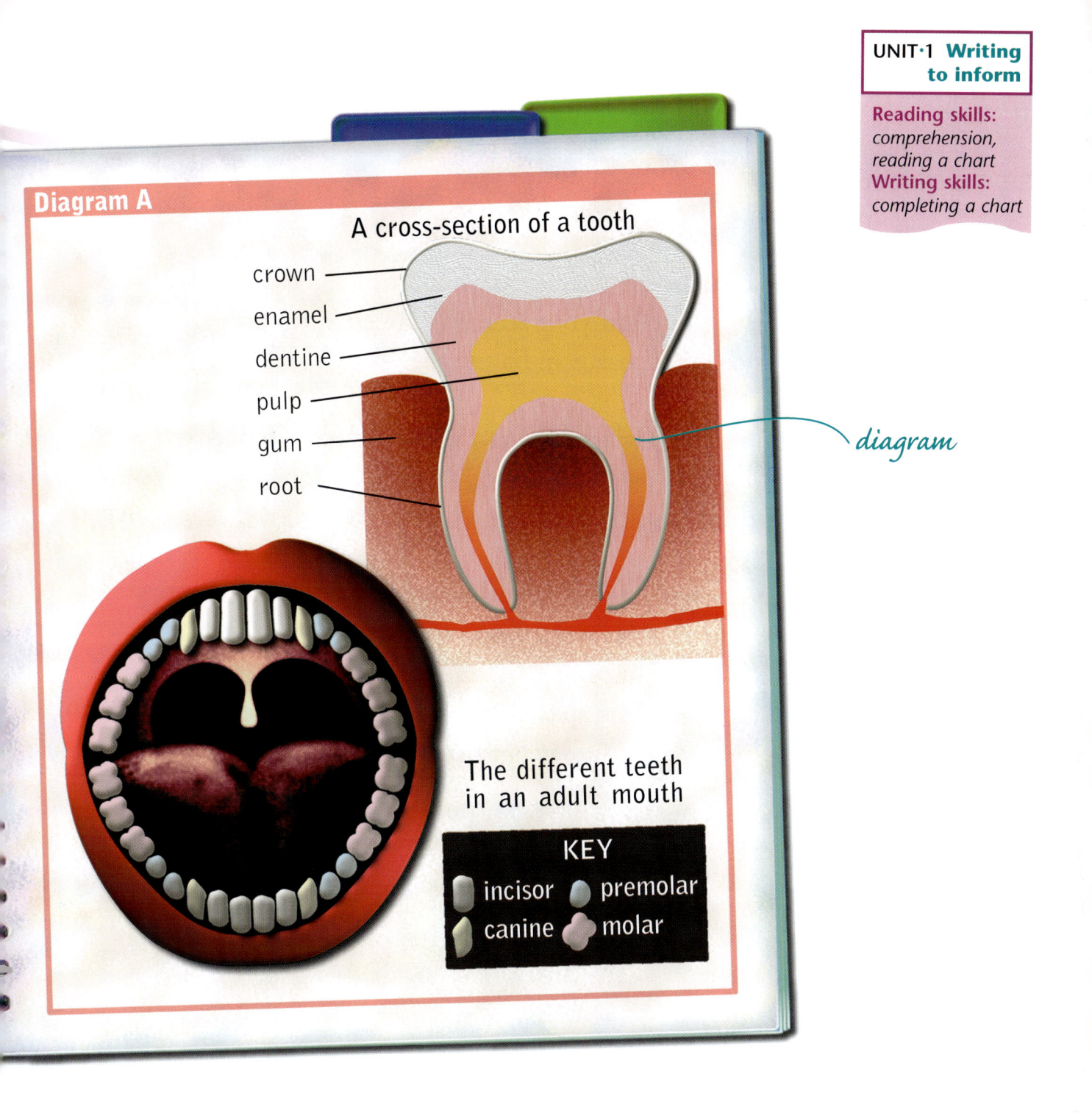

The different teeth in an adult mouth

KEY
- incisor
- premolar
- canine
- molar

3 Use the information in the report to complete the chart.

Type of tooth	Position in mouth	Number in mouth
Incisor		
Canine		4
Premolar	between the canine tooth and the molars	
Molar		

13

UNIT·1 Writing to inform

Punctuation: commas in lists

Commas in lists

Here is a **list** of things you use to clean your teeth.

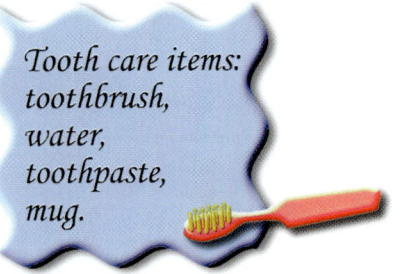

Tooth care items: toothbrush, water, toothpaste, mug.

This can also be written as a **sentence**.

EXAMPLE: To clean your teeth you need a toothbrush, water, toothpaste and a mug.

> When we write a list in a sentence we separate the items using **commas**. We don't put a comma before 'and'.

1 Write out these sentences putting in the commas.
   a The shop sold shampoo toothpaste soap and toothbrushes.
   b I love plums apricots grapes and strawberries.
   c Simon had sausages chips and beans for tea.

2 Write out the sentences, putting in the words from the lists.

*HEALTHY FOOD
apples
carrots
bread*

*UNHEALTHY FOOD FOR TEETH
Sweets
chocolate
Sugar*

   a Healthy foods for teeth are ▢ , ▢ and ▢ .
   b Foods which are bad for your teeth are ▢ , ▢ and ▢ .

3 The items in a list can be more than one word.

Today I must go to the dentist, finish my homework, walk the dog and tidy the garden.

*Things to do this week
go to dentist
walk the dog
tidy the garden*

Now write a sentence saying what you need to do this week.

Glossary
list
sentence

14

Past and present tense verbs

UNIT·1 Writing to inform
Grammar: past and present tense

The tense of a **verb** tells us when something is happening. The **present tense** tells us what is happening now. The **past tense** tells us what has already happened.

EXAMPLE: Today Sam **cleans** his teeth.
This is the **present** tense.

EXAMPLE: Yesterday Sam **cleaned** his teeth.
This is the **past** tense.

1 Write out these **sentences** adding a verb in the past or present tense.
  a Today Sam ▢ the dentist.
  b Yesterday Sam ▢ the dentist.
  c Today Allie ▢ fruit.
  d Yesterday Allie ▢ fruit.

2 Write down the present tense of these verbs.

Past tense: walked
painted
grew
pulled

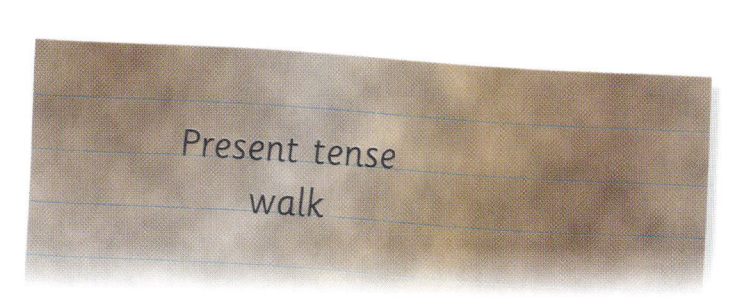

Present tense
walk

3 Change these sentences into the present tense by changing the verb.
  EXAMPLE: The boy **ran** in the rain.
  The boy **runs** in the rain.
  a He cleaned his teeth carefully.
  b They used pencils for writing.

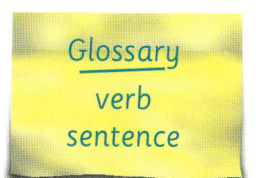

Glossary
verb
sentence

15

Writing a report

You are going to write your own report called 'Healthy teeth'.

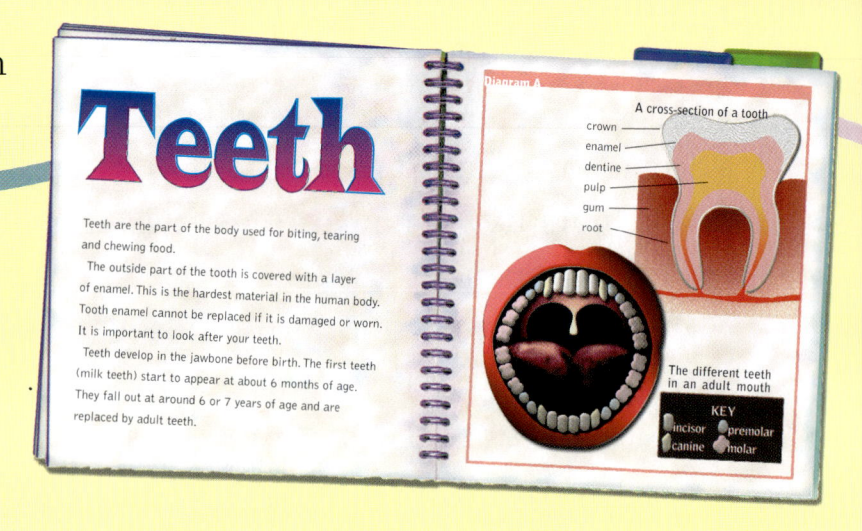

1. Reread the information on pages 12 and 13. Brainstorm all your ideas about healthy teeth.

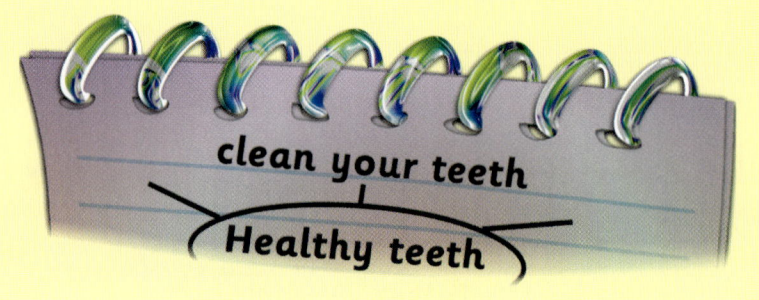

   clean your teeth
   Healthy teeth

Brainstorm

2. Make notes under these headings, using the ideas in your brainstorm web.

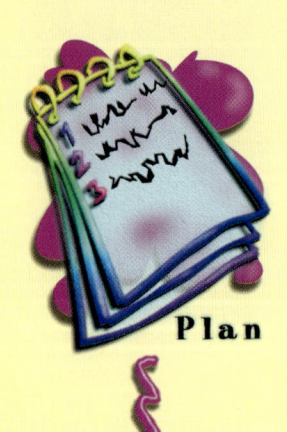

   Food and teeth

   Cleaning our teeth

   The dentist

Plan

3. Write your opening definition. This should say what healthy teeth are like and what they can do.

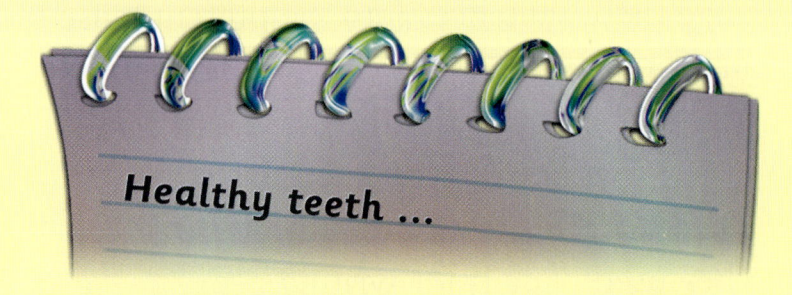

   Healthy teeth ...

16

UNIT·1 Writing to inform

4 Now use these headings to help you write a draft of your report about healthy teeth.

> ### Healthy teeth
>
> Healthy teeth are . . .
>
> To keep your teeth healthy you need to do several things.
>
> #### Food
>
> We eat . . .
>
> We should not eat . . .
>
> #### Cleaning our teeth
>
> #### Other things to keep teeth healthy

Draft

5 Swap your first draft with a friend. Get them to say which parts they think are good and how you could improve your report.

Revise

6 Make any changes that will improve your report. Then check the capital letters, full stops and question marks.

7 Think about how you are going to illustrate your report. Does it need a diagram?

8 Complete your final version.

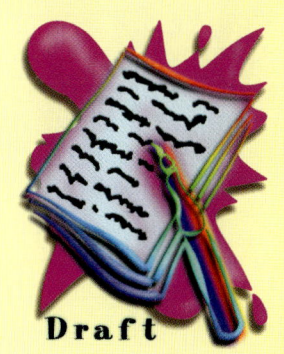

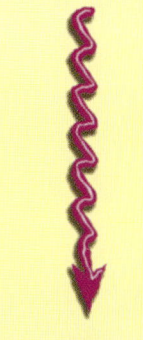

Publish

UNIT 2

Writing to entertain

In this unit you will study how to write a story. You will look at how the author starts a story to make it interesting. At the end of the unit you will plan, draft and revise your own story.

Look at how the author begins this story so that it will be interesting and exciting.

Chapter 1

Does this sentence catch your interest? — "Your Auntie Betty has copped it," said Pa Hedgehog to Ma.

"Oh no!" cried Ma. "Where?"

"Just down the road. Opposite the newsagent's. Bad place to cross, that."

characters in the story — "Everywhere's a bad place to cross nowadays," said Ma. "The traffic's dreadful. Do you realize, Pa, that's the third this year, and all on my side of the family too. First there was Grandfather, then my second cousin once removed and now poor old Auntie Betty..."

settings — They were sitting in a flower-bed at their home, the garden of Number 5A of a row of semi-detached houses in a suburban street. On the other side of the road was a park, very popular with local hedgehogs on account of the good hunting it offered. As well as worms and slugs and snails, which they could find in

6

UNIT·2 **Writing to entertain**

Text features: narrative openings, character, setting, plot

As you read, think about:
- who the story is about
- where the story is taking place
- whether the story is happening now or a long time ago
- what the main problem is for the hedgehogs
- what will happen later in the story.

their own gardens, there were special attractions in the park. Mice lived under the bandstand, feasting on the crumbs dropped from listeners' sandwiches; frogs dwelt in the lily-pond, and in the ornamental gardens grass snakes slithered through the shrubbery. All these creatures were regarded as great delicacies by the hedgehogs, and they could never resist the occasional night's sport in the park. But to reach it, they had to cross the busy road.

clue to the plot

from *The Hodgeheg* by Dick King-Smith

19

UNIT·2 Writing to entertain

Reading skills: comprehension
Vocabulary

Character and settings

1 Reread the passage from *The Hodgeheg* on pages 18 and 19.

2 Copy and complete this chart.

Title: The Hodgeheg
The **author's** name:
Characters introduced:
Setting 1:
Setting 2:

who is in the story — Characters

where the story is happening — Setting 1, Setting 2

when this might have happened

3 Write the answers to these questions about the story.
   a Pa and Ma Hedgehog lived in
      a house?   a garden?   a shop?
   b Auntie Betty was killed
      in the park?   hunting worms?   crossing the road?
   c List three things the hedgehogs ate in the garden.
   d List three things the hedgehogs ate in the park.
   e Why do you think Auntie Betty was crossing the road?

4 Find these words in the story. What you think they mean?
   Check your answers by looking up the words in a dictionary.
   a Semi-detached means
      half a house?
      two houses joined together?
      a house in the middle of a row of houses?
   b Popular means
      disliked?   liked by a lot of people?   friendly?
   c Delicacies means
      very fragile?   special foods?   friends?
   d Dwelt means
      lived?   sat?   went?

Glossary
author
character
setting

20

What happens next?

UNIT·2 Writing to entertain

Text features: *plot*

The **plot** is what happens in a story.

1 Reread the passage from *The Hodgeheg* on pages 18 and 19.

2 Talk about what you think will happen in the story. Now write a **sentence** to say what you think will happen in the story.

What I think will happen in this story
I think

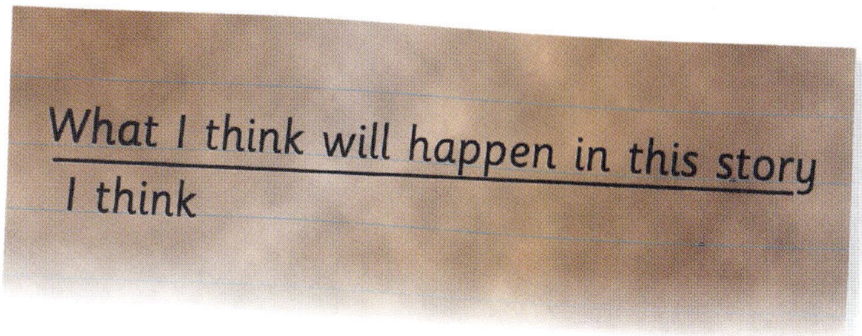

We gradually predict more of the plot as we read more of the story.

3 Read this passage from later in *The Hodgeheg*. Pa Hedgehog is talking to his children.

"Now then, you kids, just you listen to me," and he proceeded to give his children a long lecture about the problems of road safety for hedgehogs. Max listened carefully. Then he said, "Do humans cross the road?"

"I suppose so," said Pa.

"But they don't get killed?"

"Don't think so," said Pa. "Never seen one lying in the road. Which I would have if they did."

"Well then," said Max, "how do they get across safely?"

"You tell me, son. You tell me," said Pa.

"I will," said Max. "I will."

4 Now write down your new **prediction** about what will happen in the story.

5 Discuss whether your predictions about the story have changed.

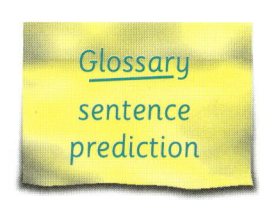

Glossary
sentence
prediction

UNIT·2 Writing to entertain

Grammar: common nouns

Nouns

Nouns are words which name things, people, places and ideas.
EXAMPLES: The **cat** ran away.   She is my **friend**.

1 Look at this picture. The **labels** are missing.
  Write a **list** of the missing labels (a, b, c, d, e, f).

The words you have used to label the picture are nouns.

2 Look around your classroom. Can you see things which could be labelled as nouns? Make a list of 8 nouns.

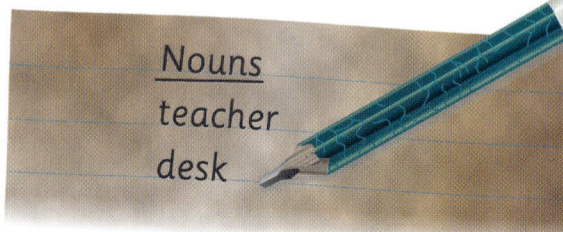

   Nouns
   teacher
   desk

3 Use nouns from your list to complete these **sentences**.
  a The _____ fell off the desk with a thump.
  b Paul tripped over a _____.
  c Don't drop the _____.
  d The teacher gave the _____ to the girl.
  e My _____ is by the window.
  f Earl had lost his _____.

4 Write a detailed **description** of your classroom and underline the nouns.

Glossary
label
list
sentence
description
setting

Remember
A description like this could be the **setting** for a story.

22

Nouns for names

Proper nouns are words which give a name to a particular person, place or idea. Proper nouns start with a **capital letter**.
EXAMPLES: **Doris** is a black cat. I am going to **London**.

1 Make a **list** of 8 proper nouns. Use the names of people and places you know.

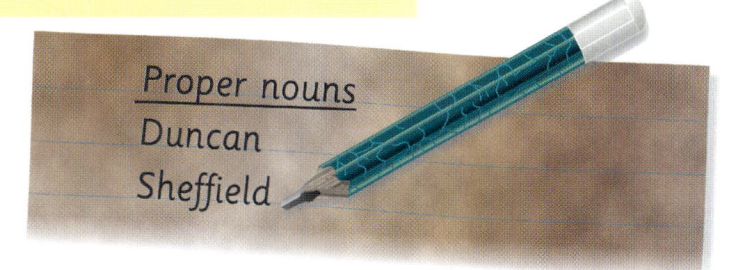

Proper nouns
Duncan
Sheffield

2 **Characters'** names are proper nouns. Write down the proper nouns in these **sentences**:
   a Once there were three baby owls: Sarah, Percy and Bill.
   b Plop was a baby barn owl and he lived with his mummy and daddy at the top of a very tall tree.

3 Sometimes the name of a character can help you imagine what they are like.
   EXAMPLE: Cruella De Vil sounds like she might be cruel because of her spiky, unusual name.
   Write a sentence to say what you think these characters are like and why you think this.
   a Goldilocks sounds like _____ because _____ .
   b Captain Pegleg sounds like _____ because _____ .
   c Prince Charming sounds like _____ because _____ .

4 Sometimes a place name can give you ideas about what it is like. Write a sentence to say what you think each of these places is like:
   a Windmill Hill   c Sunshine House
   b Milehigh Flats   d Mountainside Cottage

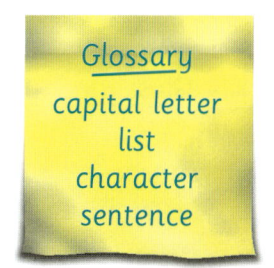

UNIT·2 **Writing to entertain**
Grammar: *proper nouns for names*

Glossary
capital letter
list
character
sentence

UNIT·2 Writing to entertain

Grammar: *adjectives*

Describing characters

Adjectives are words which tell us about **nouns**.
EXAMPLE: The big, bad wolf ate grandma up.
The adjectives **big** and **bad** describe the wolf.

1 Choose a name to fit this **character**.

2 Copy out the chart.
   Fill it in to describe the pirate in detail.

Nouns	Adjectives
hair	*black*
moustache	
hat	
eye patch	
earring	
scarf	

3 Write a **description** of the pirate to go with the poster. Use the details in your chart to help you.

4 Adjectives are used to describe characters in books so that readers can imagine them. Read these two descriptions (**A** and **B**) of Plop, the barn owl.

   A Plop was fat and fluffy.
   He had a beautiful heart-shaped ruff.
   He had enormous, round eyes.
   He had very knackety knees.

   B Plop
   He had a ruff.
   He had eyes.
   He had knees.

Glossary
noun
character
description

5 Discuss which description helps you to imagine Plop best.

6 Write down the adjectives used in description **A**.

24

Describing settings

UNIT·2 **Writing to entertain**
Grammar: *adjectives*

> **Adjectives** can also describe places and times.
> EXAMPLES: A **gloomy** house. (place) A **rainy** night. (time)

1 Write out these **sentences** putting in an adjective from the **list**.
  a The three bears lived in a _____ cottage.
  b The _____ manor house was haunted.
  c The old school was replaced with a _____ building.
  d The _____ man could touch the ceiling.
  e She wore a _____ coat to keep out the cold.
  f The bike was packed in a _____ box.

Adjective list
tall
small
gloomy
new
large
warm

2 Here are some notes which describe these two places.

big window
sweets
closed
quiet street
old-fashioned

  a Write four sentences describing each of these **settings**.
  b Give each place a suitable name.

hot
sun
fallen trees
tangled vines
noisy
birds
insects
overgrown

3 Rewrite these sentences replacing the adjectives so that the places sound different.
  EXAMPLE: It was a bright, sunny day.
            It was a wet, rainy day.
  a He crossed the busy, main road.
  b The ship sailed on the calm, smooth sea.
  c The quiet, gentle wind blew over him.
  d I climbed the tall, sturdy tree.
  e I have a clean, tidy bedroom.

Glossary
sentence
list
setting

25

Story plot

You are now going to look more closely at the **events** in a story and the way they are organized.

A story blurb

Some books contain a **blurb** at the front or on the back cover. The blurb below gives a short **account** of the story.

THE OWL WHO WAS AFRAID OF THE DARK

by Jill Tomlinson

"You can't be afraid of the dark," said the mother owl. "Owls are never afraid of the dark."

"This one is," said her young son Plop. "I want to be a day bird."

"Oh dear," said Mrs Barn Owl. She shut her eyes and, like all good mothers everywhere, tried to think how best she could help her child not to be afraid.

"You are only afraid of the dark," she said, "because you don't know about it," and sent Plop down to talk with all sorts of people on the ground below.

"Dark is exciting," said a little boy on Bonfire Day, "Dark is fun," said a boy scout guarding a camp-fire, and "Dark is wonderful," said an astronomer. In fact there wasn't one single person who didn't like the dark, but it made no difference to poor Plop; he was still scared of it – until he talked it over with another animal, a black, night-walking cat.

1 Answer these questions.
   a What was Plop afraid of?
   b Who was worried about Plop?
   c What does 'astronomer' mean?
   d List three people Plop talked to.
   e Who helped Plop not to be afraid?

2 Reread the blurb. Make a flow diagram like this.

introduction ▶ events ▶ conclusion

Glossary
event
account

26

UNIT·2 **Writing to entertain**

Reading skills: comprehension
Text features: blurbs, story sequence, chronological order

Events in order

A story contains **events**. The order in which the events happen is called the **chronological order**.

a   b   c   d

1 Write a **sentence** about each picture, using the words below to show the order of events.

   a First ...   b Next ...   c Then ...   d Finally ...

Here is a story just as Simon told it.

> In the end I climbed out of the river safely. Mind you, I was muddy and Mum was cross with me. I tripped and fell by the river. I slithered down the bank screaming "Help, help!" It all started when I ran off on my own to play by the river, even though I knew it was dangerous.

This **account** is interesting but it would be a clearer story if it was told in the order in which it happened. This is called chronological order.

2 Draw a flow chart to show the order of events as they happened to Simon.

introduction → events → conclusion

How does the story start?   What happened next?   How does the story end?

Glossary
event
sentence
account

3 Now rewrite Simon's story with a proper time sequence. Include as much detail as you can.

27

UNIT·2 Writing to entertain

Text features: *direct speech*

Characters speaking

We often know about **characters** because of what they say. This is called **direct speech**.

1 Look carefully at this cartoon and read the text below.

- "I see an open window," said Bert the burglar.
- "Carefully does it," he said as he climbed in.
- "I'll just take these lovely things out," mumbled Bert as he climbed out of the window.
- "Arrgh!" yelled Bert as a hand grabbed him.

2 What is the burglar saying? Write down what should go in each one of the four **speech bubbles** (a, b, c, d).

3 Read this conversation.
- "What are you up to?" said the policeman.
- "Just cleaning the windows," said Bert.
- "Come with me," said the policeman.
- "Oh no," said Bert.

4 Draw four cartoon pictures to show what happens. Put in speech bubbles to show exactly what is said.

5 What do you think happens next? Continue the cartoon strip with your partner.

Glossary
character
speech bubble

28

UNIT·2 **Writing to entertain**

Punctuation: *speech marks*

Writing down talk

When we write down speech we put **speech marks** around what is actually said. Any **punctuation** that goes with the speech, like **full stops**, **question marks** and **exclamation marks**, go inside the speech marks.
EXAMPLE: "The hamster has escaped!" said the teacher.

1 Write out the **sentences**. Put what the children actually said inside the speech marks.
 a "▉," said Aysha.
 b Nico said, "▉."
 c "▉," said Rajiv.
 d Sue said, "▉?"

2 Write out these sentences with speech marks around what was said next.
 a Tell the teacher, said Nico.
 b We must look for him, said Sue.
 c Stand still everybody! said Rajiv.
 d Oh, he's lost, said Aysha.

AYSHA: It's empty!
NICO: The door is open.
RAJIV: The hamster's gone!
SUE: Oh no! Where is he?

NICO: Look under the desk!
AYSHA: Look in the book corner!
RAJIV: Look in the cupboards!
SUE: Look in your tray!

3 Write a sentence to show what each child above then said. The first one is done for you.
 a *"Look under the desk!" said Nico.*

Glossary
punctuation
full stop
question mark
exclamation mark
sentence

29

Writing a story

You are going to write a story, thinking about character, setting and sequence.

Here is a brainstorm of some ideas for a story.

garden
children search
alone
Guinea pig
found by the police
left out
late at night
lost

Brainstorm

1. Think about who the story will be about. Copy and complete the chart using the notes and your own ideas.

Character	Appearance	Personality	Feelings
Police Officer PC Jasmine Smith	thin and tall dark blue uniform skirt and jacket has radio and hat	kind patient cheerful	enjoys her work happy
children			
a guinea pig			

Remember
Use adjectives when you describe your character's appearance.

2. Now write a description of each character from the chart.

3. Where and when the story takes place are important. The setting is a garden. Discuss these questions with your partner.
   - Is it a front or back garden? What does it look like?
   - What time of day is it? What is the weather like?

4. Now write a detailed description of the setting for your story.

30

UNIT·2 **Writing to entertain**

Look again at the brainstorm on the opposite page. You need to sort out the sequence of the story and add the details of the characters and setting.

5 Make a plan to show the introduction, events and conclusion of the story.

introduction ▸ events ▸ conclusion

6 Add details about the characters, setting and events to your plan. Try to include these points.
   - **Characters** Names, personality, how old, male or female?
     How do they feel?
   - **Setting** When? Where is garden? Weather?
   - **Events** Why is the guinea pig there?
     What happens?
     What does the police officer do?

7 Now use your full plan to write a draft of the story. Put in plenty of details so that the reader will find your story interesting and easy to imagine.

8 Discuss your draft with a partner and make any changes.
   - Is the story easy to understand?
   - Are the characters and story setting easy to imagine?
   - Is the story exciting?
   - Could the story be better in any way?

9 Write out your story.

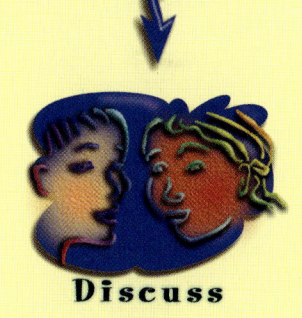

Plan

Draft

Discuss

Publish

31

UNIT·3
Writing to express

In this unit you will study how to write a list poem. You will look at how poets use language to create ideas and images in the reader's mind. At the end of the unit you will write your own list poem.

How does this opening catch your interest?

What do you notice about the start of every line?

Why do you think opposites have been used?

Why do you think these two words have been placed together?

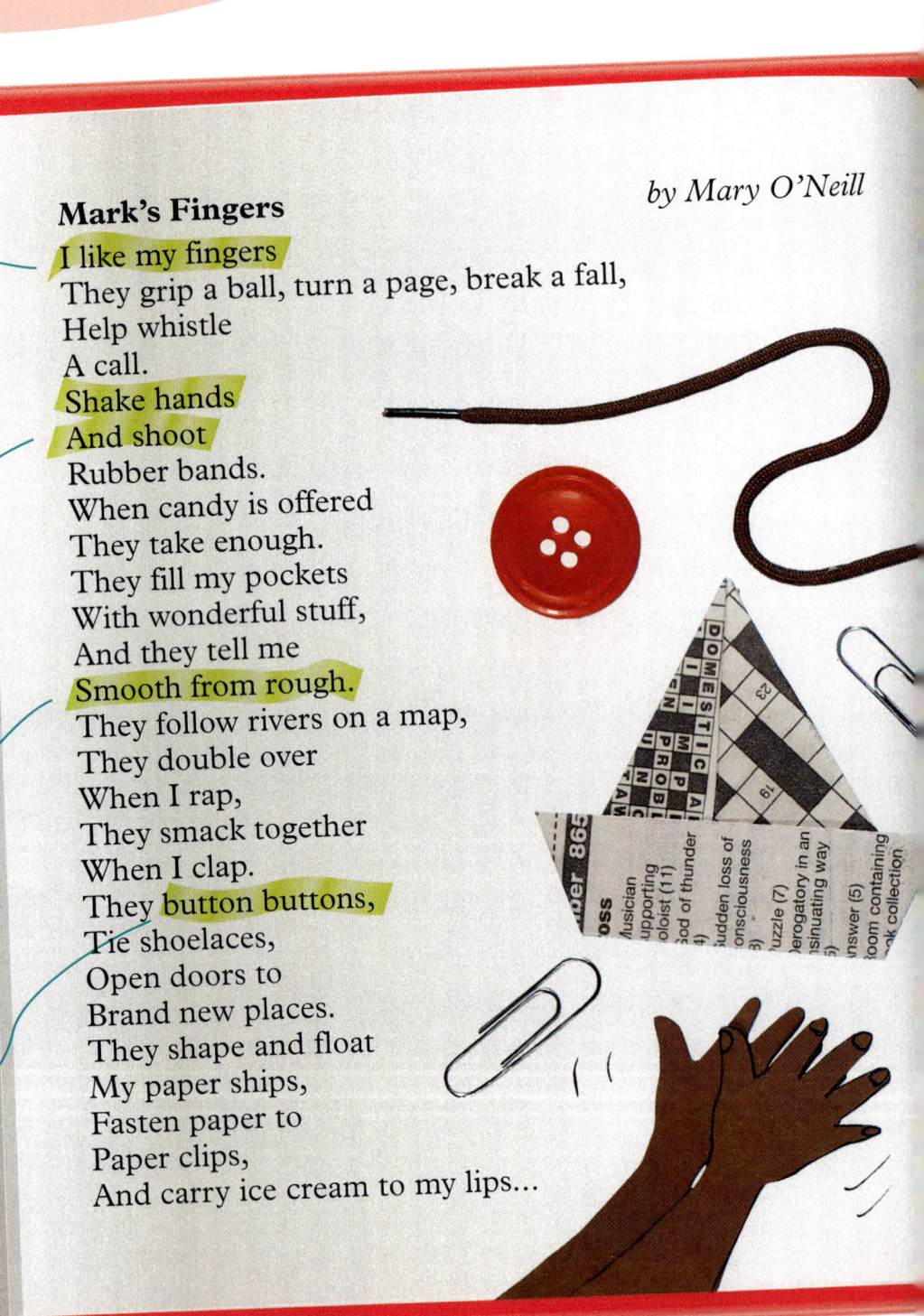

Mark's Fingers   *by Mary O'Neill*

I like my fingers
They grip a ball, turn a page, break a fall,
Help whistle
A call.
Shake hands
And shoot
Rubber bands.
When candy is offered
They take enough.
They fill my pockets
With wonderful stuff,
And they tell me
Smooth from rough.
They follow rivers on a map,
They double over
When I rap,
They smack together
When I clap.
They button buttons,
Tie shoelaces,
Open doors to
Brand new places.
They shape and float
My paper ships,
Fasten paper to
Paper clips,
And carry ice cream to my lips…

32

UNIT·3 **Writing to express**

Text features: rhyme, alliteration, imagery

Some poems use the idea of a list. But a poem is more than just a list. A poet chooses words with great care.

- Who is talking in the poem?
- Is the action taking place now, yesterday or tomorrow?
- Do all the lines rhyme?
- Why does the poem begin like it does?
- Why does the poem end like it does?

33

UNIT·3 Writing to express

Reading skills: comprehension
Words: rhyme

Using words

1 Read the poem 'Mark's Fingers' again. Answer these questions about the poem.
   a In the poem, the word 'candy' means
      a dog?   crisps?   sweets?
   b Mark's fingers 'shape and float'
      modelling clay?   paper ships?   ice?
   c List four things that fingers can do in the poem.
   d In the poem which word rhymes with hands?
   e What happens to Mark's fingers when he claps?

> There are many words in the poem that **rhyme**.
> The ends of words which rhyme sound the same.
> EXAMPLE: **race** and **place**
> They do not have to be spelt the same.
> EXAMPLE: **bean** and **seen**

2 Copy and complete this chart. Find the rhyming words in the poem to complete Column A.
   The first one has been done for you.

Word from the poem	Column A Other rhyming words in the poem	Column B Other words which rhyme with the words in Column A
ball	fall, call	hall, small
hands		
map		
enough		
shoelaces		
ships		

3 Now add as many other rhyming words as you can think of to go in Column B.

34

Verbs

> The poem 'Mark's Fingers' lists a lot of different things his fingers can do.
>
> EXAMPLE: They **grip** a ball, **turn** a page, **break** a fall. Grip, turn and break are all **verbs**. A verb is a word which tells us what people or objects are doing or being. Most **sentences** contain a verb.

Verbs
clap

1 Write out five verbs from the poem that tell you what Mark's fingers do.

2 Put four of the verbs into new sentences.
   EXAMPLE: I button my school shirt every morning when I get dressed.

3 Our feet do lots of different things, just like our fingers. What are the children in this picture doing with their feet? Write a sentence to describe what each child, or pair of children, is doing in the picture.
   EXAMPLE: Sam *is kicking a football to Mary.*
   a Lucy ...
   b Elif ...
   c Jenny ...
   d Cheng ...
   e Alex and Darren ...

4 Underline the main verb in each sentence above.
   EXAMPLE: Sam is <u>kicking</u> a football to Mary.

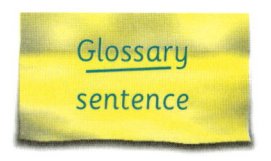

UNIT·3 Writing to express

Grammar: verbs

Glossary
sentence

UNIT·3 Writing to express

Words: *alliteration*

Using sounds

1 Read this **list** poem. It lists what someone would like to have in their house.

Cottage
by Eleanor Farjeon

When I live in a cottage
I shall keep in my cottage
Two different dogs,
Three creamy cats,
Four giddy goats,
Five pewter pots,
Six silver spoons,
Seven busy beehives,
Eight ancient apple trees,
Nine red rose bushes
Ten teeming teapots,
Eleven chirping chickens,
Twelve cosy cats with their kittenish kittens and
One blessèd baby in a basket.
That's what I'll have when I live in my cottage.

What do you notice about these **nouns** and **adjectives**? When several words begin with the same **consonant** we call this **alliteration**.
EXAMPLES: **g**iddy **g**oats, **p**ewter **p**ots, **c**osy **c**ats

Remember
You can use alliteration when you write your own poem.

2 Write an alliterative **sentence** for your name, your friend's name and your teacher's name.
EXAMPLES: Satwinder slowly sips her squash.
Mrs Lewis loves lemon lollipops.

3 In this shopping list some words have been hidden. Use alliteration to fill in the missing words.

five ▬ fish
six ▬ sausages
two tins of ▬
four ▬ fruits

Glossary
list
noun
adjective
consonant
sentence

4 Write your own alliterative list of six things you would like to have in your bedroom.

I would like
a bouncy bed
a

36

Where things are

1 Here is another list poem. In pairs, read it to each other.

Cats
by Eleanor Farjeon

Cats sleep
Anywhere,
Any table
Any chair,
Top of piano,
Window-ledge,
In the middle,
On the edge
Open drawer,
Empty shoe,
Anybody's
Lap will do,
Fitted in a cardboard box,
In the cupboard
With your frocks -
Anywhere!
They don't care!
Cats sleep
Anywhere.

This list poem tells you where cats like to sleep. Words that tell you the position of something are called **prepositions**.

EXAMPLES: **on** pianos, **in** cupboards

in   on   next   alongside   down   into
under   above   to   over   behind   off
through   near   by   between

2 Write a list of five places where a dog might sleep. Choose from the prepositions above.

EXAMPLE: Dogs sleep alongside the radiator.

3 Write a **description** of your classroom which tells the reader where things are.

4 Underline all the prepositions you have used.

UNIT·3 Writing to express
Grammar: prepositions

Glossary
description

37

Words in a list poem

You are now going to look closely at how we can use words to create pictures in our heads.

Similes

This poem lists what the different shoes look like. 'Mark's Fingers' listed the things his fingers could do.

Shoes *by John Foster*

Red shoes, blue shoes,
Old shoes, new shoes,
Shoes that are black,
Shoes that are white,
Shoes that are loose,
Shoes that are tight.
Shoes with buckles,
Shoes with bows,
Shoes that are narrow
And pinch your toes.
Shoes that are yellow,
Shoes that are green,
Shoes that are dirty,
Shoes that are clean.
Shoes for cold weather,
Shoes for when it's hot.
Shoes with laces
That get tangled in a knot.

Colour list
red

1 The 'Shoes' poem uses lots of colour words.
   Make a list of all the colours mentioned in the poem.

> Instead of just saying the colour, writers and poets often compare the colour to something else.
> EXAMPLES: '**as** red **as** the setting sun'   'red **like** a fire'
> These ways of comparing one thing with another are called **similes**.

Remember
You can use similes when you write your own list poem.

2 Write a simile for each of these colours.
   Use either 'as' or 'like'.
   EXAMPLES: *as green as grass* or *green like grass*
   a as orange as …   c white like a …
   b yellow like a …   d as brown as …

3 Write a simile for each of these feelings:
   a happy   b sad   c angry   d proud   e timid

Antonyms

UNIT·3 Writing to express

Words: similes, antonyms

The poem 'Shoes' compares shoes that are very different from each other. Comparing things helps us to build an image in our minds.

EXAMPLES: **loose** shoes – **tight** shoes
old shoes – **new** shoes

Loose and tight, old and new are words with opposite meanings. Words with opposite meanings are called **antonyms**.

1 Copy out and match these antonyms (opposites). The first one is done for you.

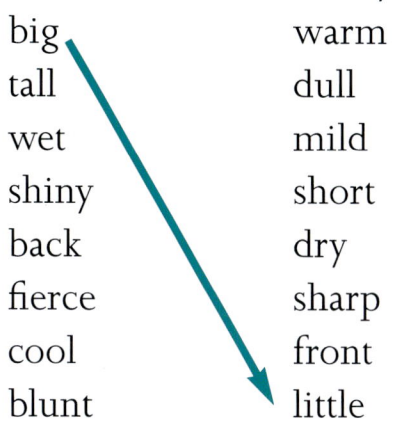

big	warm
tall	dull
wet	mild
shiny	short
back	dry
fierce	sharp
cool	front
blunt	little

2 Write an antonym (opposite) for these **verbs**:
   a pull   **b** run   **c** shout   **d** cry   **e** love

3 Write an antonym for these **nouns**:
   a friend
   b countryside
   c day
   d giant
   e mountain

4 Think of a pair of antonyms and illustrate them. See if a friend can add the correct words.

Remember
You can compare things that are opposites when you write your **list** poem.

Glossary
verb
noun
list

UNIT·3 Writing to express

Words: categorization, compound words

More words

In the poem on page 38 the poet repeats the **noun** 'shoes' many times to make us notice it. There are also many other words that we use to name different kinds of footwear.

EXAMPLES: **sandals**, **boots**, **slippers**

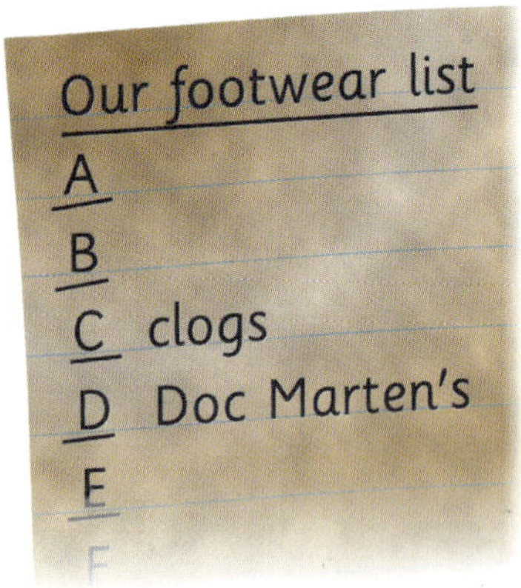

1 Make a **list** of all the 'footwear' words you know.

2 Compare your lists and make a group list arranged in **alphabetical order**. You may not have a word for every letter of the alphabet.

Our footwear list
A
B
C clogs
D Doc Marten's
E
F

We often use one word to name a group of things.
EXAMPLE: trainers, slippers and clogs are all footwear. We say this is a **category** of objects

3 Add as many objects as you can to these categories.
  a furniture: table, ...   c drinks: water, ...
  b fruit: apple, ...   d vehicles: car, ...

The word 'shoelaces' is used in both 'Mark's Fingers' and 'Shoes'. Shoelace is a **compound word** because it is made of two words joined together. Both parts of the word make sense on their own.
EXAMPLE: shoe + lace = shoelace.

4 Work out what these compound words are from the picture clues.
  a   b 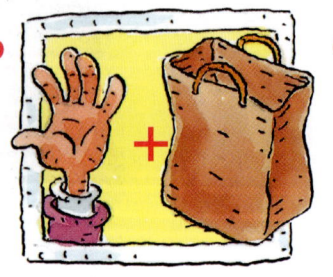   c

Glossary
noun
list
alphabetical
order

5 Think of a compound word and draw a picture clue for it using two pictures. See if a friend can work out what the word is.

40

UNIT·3 Writing to express

Grammar
singular and plural nouns

One and more than one

We talk and write about one shoelace or two shoelaces. When we mean one thing, it is **singular**.

EXAMPLE: **shoelace**

When we mean more than one thing, it is **plural**.

EXAMPLE: **shoelaces**

Plural rules
Rule 1
Most nouns add an 's' to become plural.

1 Copy these **nouns**, making them into plurals by adding an 's'.

a	one shoe	two …	d	a ball	several …
b	a finger	five …	e	my slipper	both …
c	the map	two …	f	one bag	some …

2 Look at the plural of these nouns that end in 'y'. They all follow the same rule. Work out the rule.

EXAMPLES: fairy – fairies, city – cities, story – stories, baby – babies, factory – factories

3 Now complete this **sentence**.

Rule 2
For most nouns that end in the letter 'y' you should

4 Use the two rules to change the nouns in this passage from singular to plural. All the highlighted words need changing.

The friend ran down the road. They wanted to get to the shop before closing time. Chen wanted a bag of sweet and Sam wanted a book of story. They wanted to buy present for Mary's birthday party. "Here's a good book," said Chen. When they had chosen their gift they also bought birthday card and two sheet of wrapping paper. "Now we've got all the thing we need" said Chen.

Glossary
noun
sentence

41

UNIT·3 Writing to express

Punctuation: *commas*

Commas in lists

We often make **lists** to help us remember things.

tidy bedroom
phone Gran
do homework
return library book

bread
sugar
tea
milk

> When we write a list in a **sentence** we separate the items using **commas**.
>
> EXAMPLES: From the supermarket I need bread**,** sugar**,** tea and milk.
>
> I must tidy my bedroom**,** phone Gran**,** do my homework and return my library book.
>
> The last two items in the list are joined by the word 'and' instead of a comma.

1 Here are some supermarket bills.

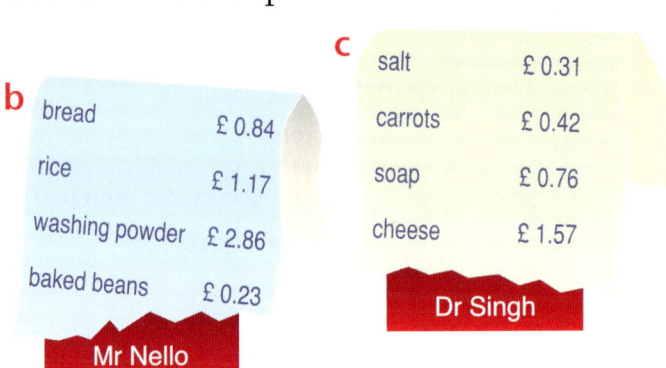

a Mrs Jones
apples	£ 0.76
bananas	£ 0.63
cat food	£ 1.24
squash	£ 0.98

b Mr Nello
bread	£ 0.84
rice	£ 1.17
washing powder	£ 2.86
baked beans	£ 0.23

c Dr Singh
salt	£ 0.31
carrots	£ 0.42
soap	£ 0.76
cheese	£ 1.57

d Mrs McGregor
shampoo	£ 1.83
pasta	£ 1.25
biscuits	£ 0.66
crisps	£ 0.28

Write a sentence saying what each person bought. Put in the commas between each item. The first one has been started for you.

   a Mrs Jones bought a bottle of squash, apples, ...

2 Put five items in each list.

   My favourite foods   Girls' names   Dogs' names

3 Now change each list into a sentence.

4 Put the commas into these sentences.
   a For my holiday I need a bottle of sun tan cream a swimsuit a sun hat and an umbrella.
   b Go to the shops and buy two oranges a tin of dog food a box of fish fingers and a cauliflower.

Remember
Use commas to separate the items in a sentence.

Glossary
list
sentence

42

Conjunctions

> On the last page you saw that the final two words of a list in a **sentence** are joined together by the word '**and**'. Words that join sentences or parts of sentences together are called **conjunctions**.

Here are two sentences about the painting:

> The man is happy. He is smiling.

We can join these two sentences together in different ways.

EXAMPLES: The man is happy and he is smiling.
 The man is happy so he is smiling.
 Because the man is happy he is smiling.

This famous painting is called The Laughing Cavalier

1 Talk about whether the three sentences have different meanings.

Here are some more conjunctions.

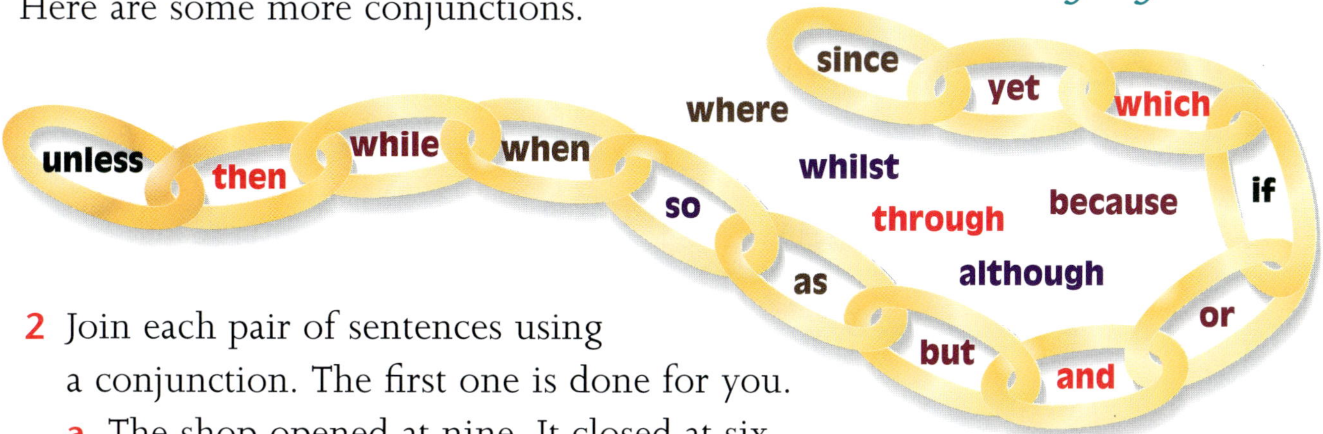

unless, then, while, when, where, since, yet, which, so, whilst, through, because, if, as, although, but, and, or

2 Join each pair of sentences using a conjunction. The first one is done for you.
   a The shop opened at nine. It closed at six.
      The shop opened at nine and it closed at six.
   b The children were swimming. The water was cold.
   c The cat was hungry. The children fed it.
   d The sky was grey. The clouds hid the sun.
   e It was raining. She took an umbrella.
   f It was still cold. It was sunny.
   g The bus waited. She ran to catch it.

Remember
When you join sentences with a conjunction you make one new sentence.

3 Discuss your new sentences with a partner. Have you chosen the same conjunction for each sentence? Do your sentences have different meanings?

Glossary
sentence

Writing a list poem

You have looked at several list poems in this unit. Now you are going to write your own list poem about a part of your body.

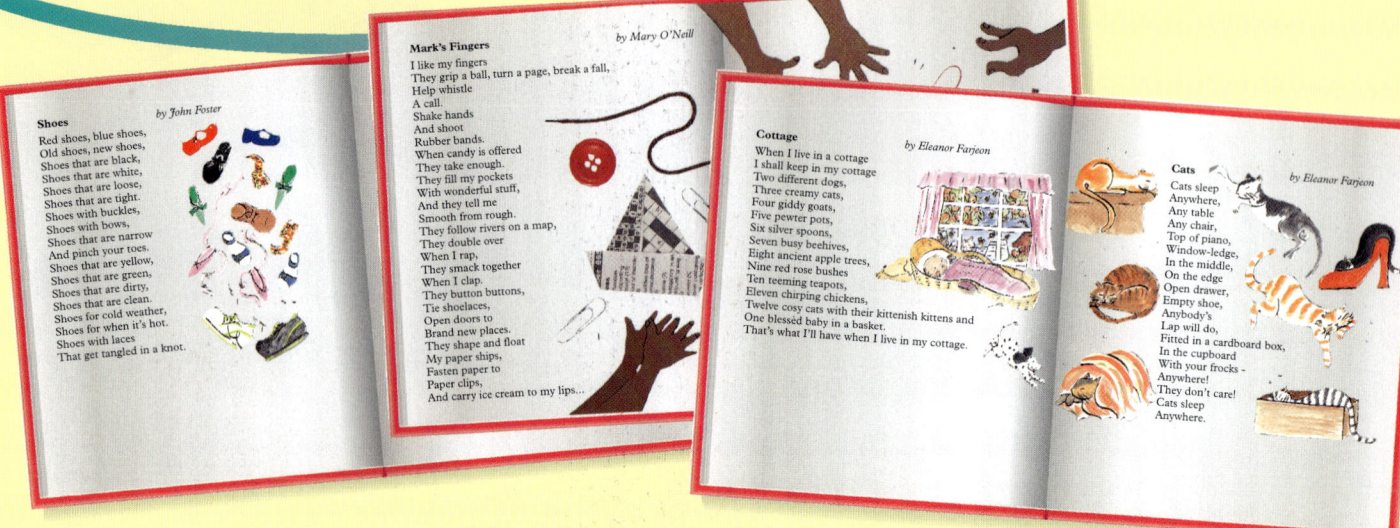

1 Reread 'Mark's Fingers' (page 32) and any other list poems you have liked.

2 Select the part of the body you want to write about.

3 Brainstorm things you do with that part of the body.

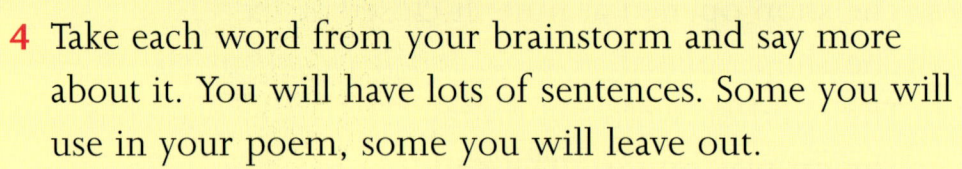

Brainstorm

eat, smile, talk, laugh, shout, suck, argue, whisper, sing, chew

4 Take each word from your brainstorm and say more about it. You will have lots of sentences. Some you will use in your poem, some you will leave out.

EXAMPLE: smile

Plan

- My mouth smiles slowly when I'm happy.
- My mouth smiles broadly when my teacher says well done.
- My mouth smiles politely when I visit my aunty.

44

UNIT·3 Writing to express

5   Work on the language of each of the sentences you have written. Try lots of different ideas.
   - Try adding alliteration.
     EXAMPLE: My mouth smiles in a wide welcoming way.
   - Try adding similes.
     EXAMPLE: My mouth can whisper like gentle breezes in the leaves.
   - Try adding opposites for contrast, e.g. whisper/roar.
     EXAMPLE: My mouth can roar like the largest football crowd.
   - Try adding adjectives.
     EXAMPLE: My open rounded mouth.

6   Your opening statement is important. You must decide which of your ideas will attract the reader's attention.

7   Now write a first draft using your opening statement and the sentences you like best.

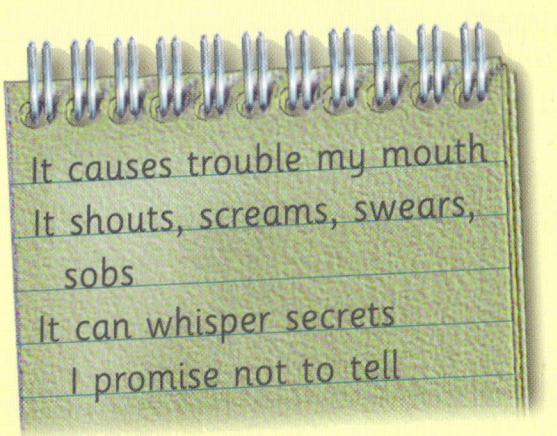

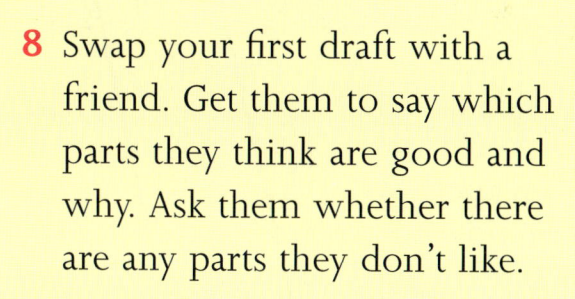

Draft

It causes trouble my mouth
It shouts, screams, swears, sobs
It can whisper secrets
   I promise not to tell

I like my mouth
My mouth smiles
My mouth laughs

8   Swap your first draft with a friend. Get them to say which parts they think are good and why. Ask them whether there are any parts they don't like.

9   Make any alterations that will improve your poem.

10 Copy out your final draft and mount it on a piece of paper in the shape of the body part.

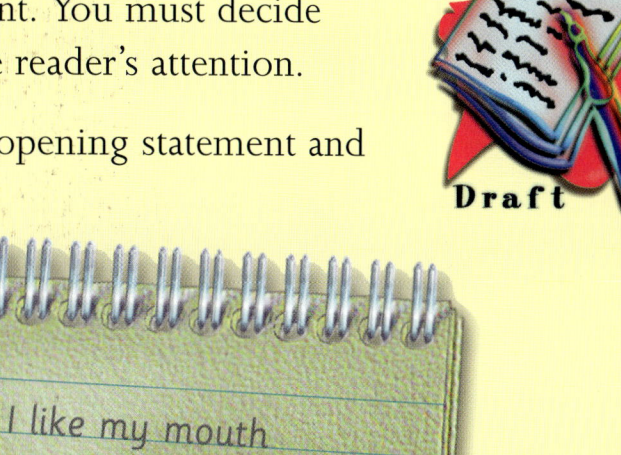

Publish

45

UNIT·4
Writing to instruct

In this unit you will study how instructions are written.
Instructions tell us how to do or make something.
At the end of the unit you will write
a set of instructions.

statement of goal —

How to make a spinner

Things you need
Piece of thick paper or card (18 cm x 12 cm)
paper clip
ruler
pencil
scissors

What to do

1 First draw two parallel unbroken lines from the bottom of the short side of the card. Each line should be 12 cm long, 4 cm apart and 4 cm from each side.

precise information —

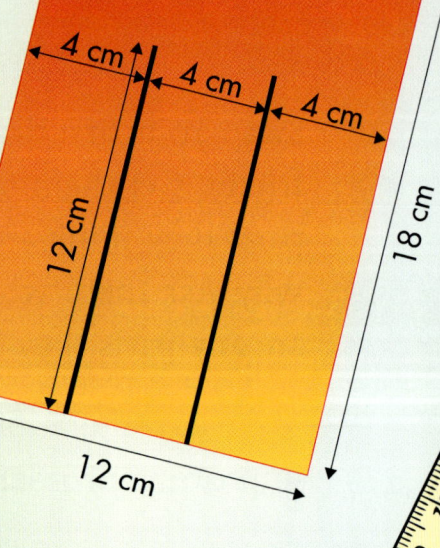

46

UNIT·4 Writing to instruct

Text features: goal, materials, steps

- What is the aim of these instructions?
- Why is there a list of the things you need at the beginning?
- Why are the instructions given in order?
- Why are diagrams used?
- Who are the instructions written for?

command

2 Next draw two dotted lines starting from the sides of the card and meeting at the top of the unbroken lines. They should each be 4 cm long.

3 Now cut along the unbroken lines.

linking word to do with time

4 Then fold along the dotted lines to make the 'vanes'.

technical names

vane

5 Clip the paper clip to the bottom of the central vane to add weight.

6 Finally, throw the spinner into the air. Watch it fall.

83

47

UNIT·4 Writing to instruct

Reading skills: *comprehension*
Words: *abbreviations*

Remember
Answer your questions in sentences.

Comprehension

1. Reread the **instructions** 'How to make a spinner' on page 47. Answer these questions about the passage.
    a. To make the weight you need
        a piece of clay?   a ball bearing?   a paper clip?
    b. You have to draw
        two lines?   four lines?   six lines?
    c. Why do you throw the spinner up into the air?

2. Look closely at the words and pictures. Now answer these questions about the words in the passage.
    a. The words 'parallel lines' mean
        lines the same distance apart?   lines which cross?
        a circle?
    b. The word 'vanes' means
        the wheels of a helicopter?   the helicopter blades?
        a part of an aeroplane?
    c. List four **nouns** from the 'Things you need' section.
    d. Name the **adjective** in the 'Things you need' section.

Abbreviations

The instructions for 'How to make a spinner' use a short way to write some words.
EXAMPLE: cm = centimetres
These shortened ways of writing words are called **abbreviations**.

Remember
Use your dictionary to look up word meanings.

Glossary
instructions
noun
adjective

1. Instructions often use abbreviations for units of measurement. Match the abbreviations to the units of measurement. The first one is done for you.

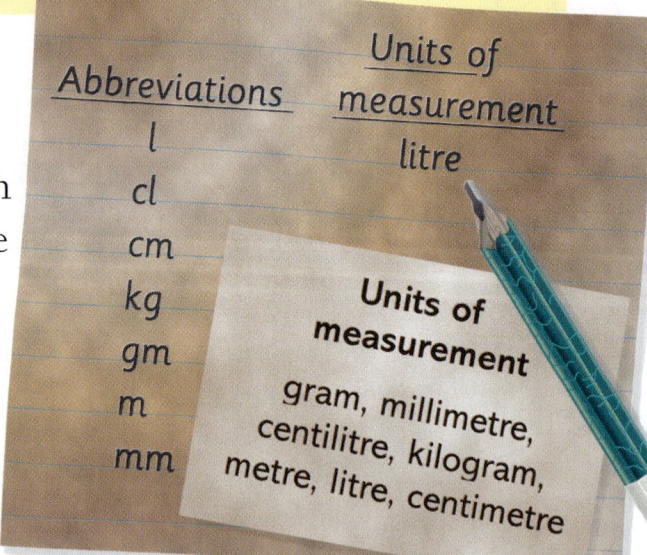

Abbreviations	Units of measurement
l	litre
cl	
cm	
kg	
gm	
m	
mm	

Units of measurement
gram, millimetre, centilitre, kilogram, metre, litre, centimetre

48

Events in order

'How to make a spinner' on page 46 tells you what to do in time order. This is called **chronological order**. It is important to get the order of **instructions** right.

UNIT·4 Writing to instruct

Text features:
chronological order
Words:
alphabetical order

Mrs Bill left these instructions for her husband's tea.

Get the pizza out of the fridge
Put the pizza in the oven
Turn the oven on at 220°C
Leave the pizza in the oven for 10 mins
Open the box and remove the plastic wrapper
Remove the pizza from the oven.

1. What would happen if Mr Bill followed these instructions as they are written?

2. Rewrite the instructions and give each **sentence** a number.

   1 Get the pizza out of the fridge.

3. Give these instructions a **title** so that it is clear what they are for.

Remember
The title should state the aim of the instructions.

4. You can also use the letters of the alphabet to order instructions. Rearrange these instructions for withdrawing a book from the library so that they are in the correct order.

a)
   Give the book and your library ticket to the librarian.
   Take the book and library ticket and leave.
   Select the book you want.
   Wait for the librarian to record the book.
   Take the book to the counter.

Glossary
instructions
sentence
title

49

UNIT·4 Writing to instruct

Text features: *chronological connectives*

Linking words

> **Instructions** sometimes use linking words which are to do with when something should happen. These words are called **connectives**.
> EXAMPLE: **First** cut the paper. **Then** add the weight.

1. These words are some of the connectives that show the order of events. Find them in 'How to make a spinner'.
   a first **b** next **c** now **d** then **e** finally

2. In these instructions the sequence has become jumbled. Rewrite the instructions putting them in the correct **chronological order**. Use the connectives to help you.

   How to use a public telephone
   When you hear the dialling tone place the money in the slot.
   First pick up the receiver.
   Finally replace the receiver at the end of the call.
   After the money is inserted dial the number.
   Next listen for the dialling tone.
   Then listen for the ringing tone which tells you the call has got through.

Remember
Look up any words you do not understand in the dictionary.

3. In these instructions for making chocolate cornflakes the writer has used 'then' too many times. Rewrite the recipe using different words in place of 'then'.

   Chocolate Cornflakes
   Put 20 gm of cornflakes in a mixing bowl.
   Then break 150 gm chocolate into a heat-proof bowl.
   Then place the bowl of chocolate over a pan of hot water.
   When the chocolate has melted mix it in with the cornflakes.
   Then put a spoonful of the mixture into each cake case.
   Then leave to cool.

Glossary
instructions
chronological order
list
title
capital letter

4. Write a **list** of all the things you need to make chocolate cornflakes.

5. Write a **title** for the instructions.

Remember
Titles begin with a **capital letter**.

Words of command

UNIT·4 Writing to instruct

Grammar: *imperative verbs*

> Every **sentence** in 'How to make a spinner' has at least one word that tells you what to do. Words which tell the reader what to do are called **imperative verbs**.
> EXAMPLES: **tie, fold, cut**

1 Make a list of six imperative verbs from the **instructions** for making a spinner (page 46).

Imperative verbs
cut

2 Every sentence in a set of instructions needs a verb. In these instructions the verb has been missed out. Add the missing verbs.

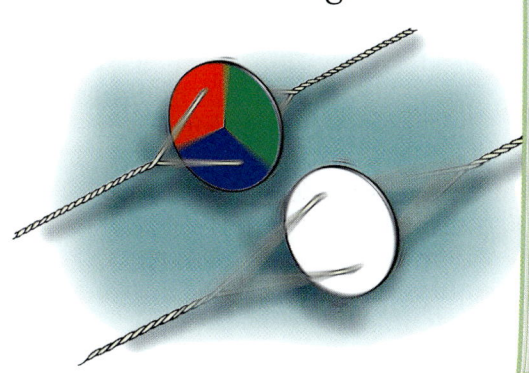

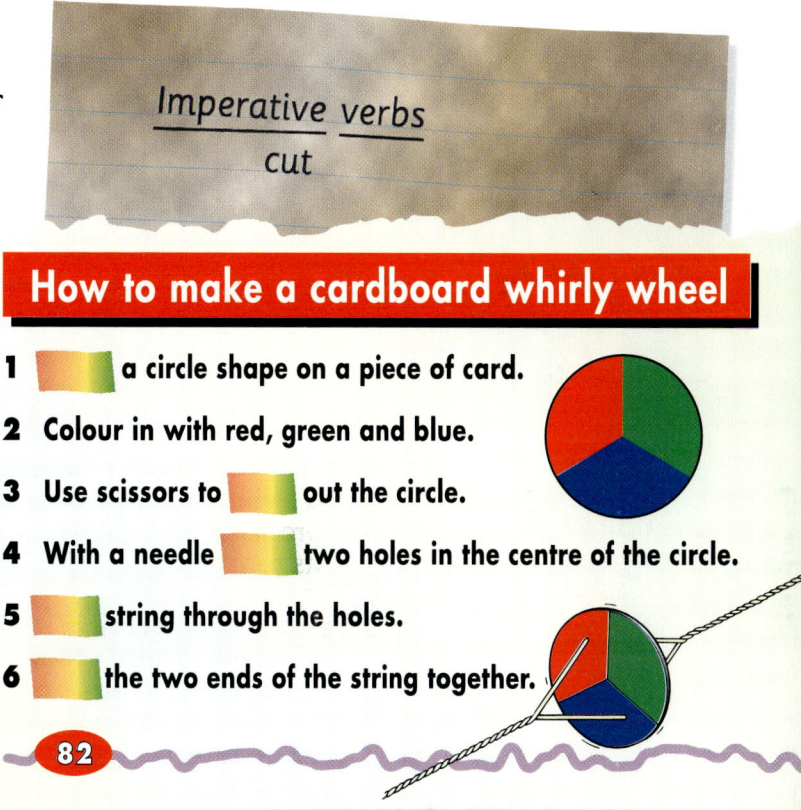

How to make a cardboard whirly wheel

1 ▭ a circle shape on a piece of card.
2 Colour in with red, green and blue.
3 Use scissors to ▭ out the circle.
4 With a needle ▭ two holes in the centre of the circle.
5 ▭ string through the holes.
6 ▭ the two ends of the string together.

82

3 When Simon tells us how he wrapped up a book he gives an **account** in the **past tense**.

> 1 First I laid the paper on the table.
> 2 Then I put the book on the paper.
> 3 Next I wrapped the paper round the book and stuck it down.
> 4 Then I tied the string around the parcel.
> 5 Finally I wrote the address on the parcel and sent it.

Change the verbs in each sentence so that they become instructions telling the reader what to do.

EXAMPLE: 1 First I laid the paper on the table.
          1 *First lay the paper on the table.*

Glossary
sentence
verb
instructions
account
past tense

51

UNIT·4 Writing to instruct
Reading skills: using a dictionary
Words: definitions

What does it mean?

The **instructions** for making a spinner (page 46) contain some special words about spinners (vane, weight). To find out more about these words you can look in a dictionary. A **dictionary entry** tells you several things about a **noun**.

1 Look at this page from a dictionary.

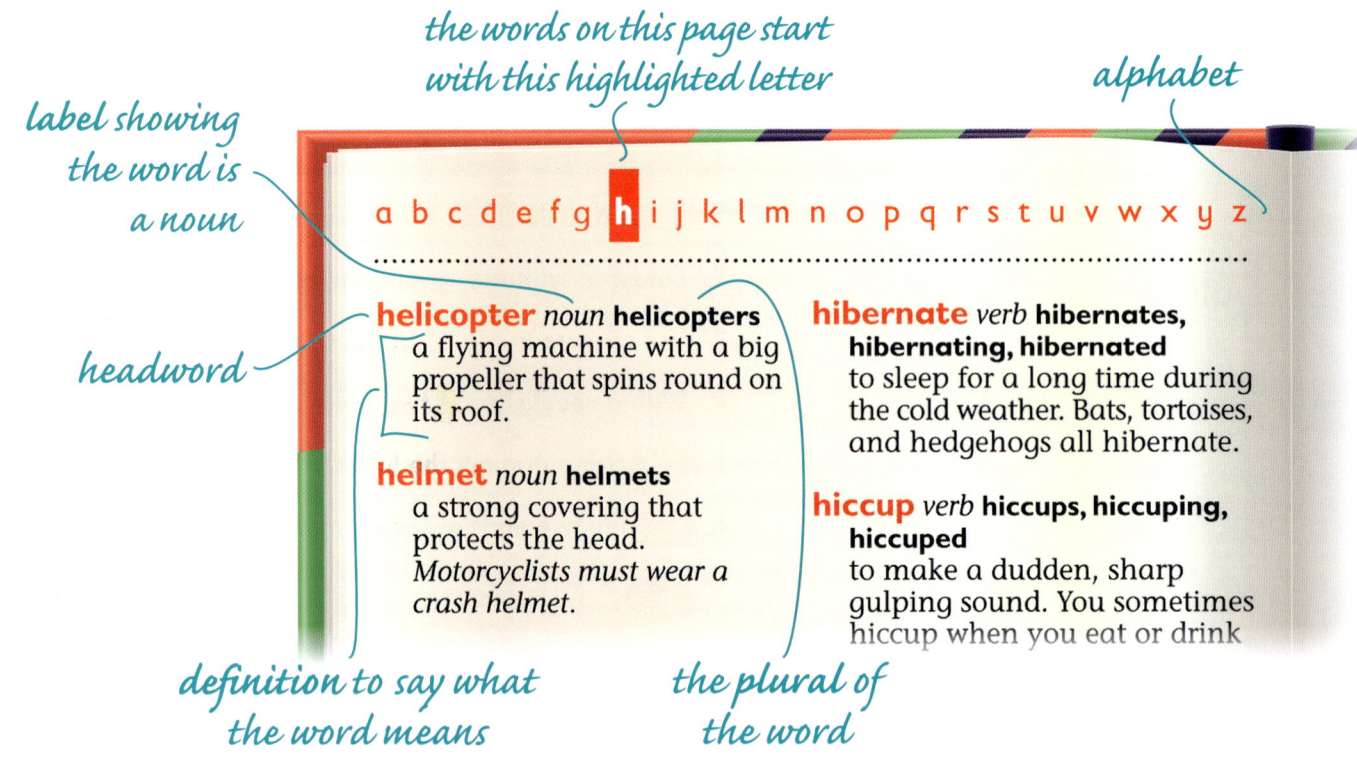

the words on this page start with this highlighted letter

alphabet

label showing the word is a noun

a b c d e f g **h** i j k l m n o p q r s t u v w x y z

headword

helicopter *noun* **helicopters**
a flying machine with a big propeller that spins round on its roof.

helmet *noun* **helmets**
a strong covering that protects the head. Motorcyclists must wear a crash helmet.

hibernate *verb* **hibernates, hibernating, hibernated**
to sleep for a long time during the cold weather. Bats, tortoises, and hedgehogs all hibernate.

hiccup *verb* **hiccups, hiccuping, hiccuped**
to make a dudden, sharp gulping sound. You sometimes hiccup when you eat or drink

definition to say what the word means

the plural of the word

2 Answer these questions.
   a What letter do all the words on this page begin with?
   b Is this page in the first or second half of the dictionary?
   c Write down the two headwords which are nouns.
   d Write down the two headwords which are **verbs**.
   e Which of these words will you find in the second half of the dictionary?

   spin   aeroplane   yacht   rocket   train   car

   f Which of these words will you find in the first half of the dictionary?

   string   ruler   materials   circle   knot   weight

Glossary
instructions
label
noun
definition
plural
verb

52

Definitions

The dictionary tells you what a word means. This is called the **definition**. Sometimes we can work out what a word means for ourselves. We can use the dictionary definition to check our definition.

1 Copy out the chart. Fill in Column A first. Then use the dictionary to fill in Column B.

	Column A My definition	Column B Dictionary definition
helicopter		
vanes		
submarine		
materials		

2 Talk about any differences between your definition and the dictionary definition.

Sometimes a word can have more than one definition. Certain activities, jobs and objects have special words that go with them.

EXAMPLES: Football words — shoot, pass, dribble, match, pitch

Computer words — mouse, keyboard, file, window

These special words can be ordinary words with a different meaning.

EXAMPLE:

mouse *noun* **mice**
1 a small furry animal with a long tail.
2 a small device you move about on your desk to control the cursor on a computer screen.

3 Give an ordinary definition and a specialist definition for three of the words from the computer list or football list.

4 Check your definitions in a dictionary.

UNIT 4 Writing to instruct
Reading skills: *using a dictionary*
Words: *definitions*

Glossary
list

More instructions

You have looked at **instructions** that tell you how to make something. Now you are going to look closely at instructions that tell you how to do something.

How to play noughts and crosses

aim —
Aim of the game
For one player to complete a row of three identical marks (either 'O' or 'X'). The rows may be in any direction – horizontal, vertical or diagonal. If no winning row is made the result is a draw.

equipment —
You will need
sheet of paper – 2 pencils – 2 players.

what to do —
How to play
1. Decide who will draw Os and who will draw Xs.
2. Draw a grid on the paper. The grid should have three rows and three columns as in the diagram.
3. Player 1 draws their mark (O or X) in any empty square of their choice.
4. Player 2 draws their mark (O or X) in any empty square of their choice.
5. The players continue to take turns to make their mark until they produce a winning line.

Hints on how to play
Think carefully before you make your mark. You must watch closely to see if your opponent has a line that is nearly complete.

Remember
Use a dictionary to look up words you are unsure of.

Glossary
instructions

1. Answer these questions about the game.
   a. The number of players in a game of noughts and crosses is
      four?   two?   three?
   b. The number of noughts or crosses in a winning line is
      four?   two?   three?
   c. What happens if no winning line is produced?
   d. Why is it important to have the word 'empty' in steps 3 and 4?
   e. Which word means 'a slanting line drawn from one corner to the opposite corner'?
   f. What does the word 'horizontal' mean?

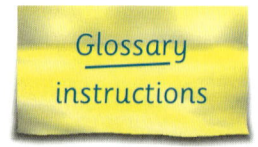

Adverbs

We can add details to **verbs** to tell the reader exactly how we want them to do something.
EXAMPLES: 'think **carefully**' and 'watch **closely**'
Both 'carefully' and 'closely' are adverbs.
Adverbs are words that give more details about the verb they are describing.

UNIT·4 **Writing to instruct**
Reading skills: *comprehension*
Grammar: *adverbs of manner*

Kate is shouting angrily.

Chan is shouting loudly.

Darren is shouting excitedly.

Have you noticed that all these adverbs end in 'ly'.

1. These three children are shouting.
   Write down the adverb in each **sentence**.

2. Make a list of all the adverbs that might go with the verb 'speak'.
   The list has been started for you.

   speak
   speak quietly
   speak slowly
   speak

3. Copy these sentences. All the verbs are highlighted.
   Write out all the adverbs which describe these verbs.
   a Write the address clearly.
   b Shout loudly so that everyone will hear.
   c Clean the cups thoroughly.
   d Drop the spinner carefully.

   Remember
   The adverb is not always right next to the verb in a sentence.

4. Change these words to adverbs by adding 'ly'
   EXAMPLE: quick + ly = quickly
   a narrow   b slow   c bad   d clever

   Glossary
   verb
   sentence

UNIT·4 **Writing to instruct**

Grammar:
exclamations
Punctuation:
exclamation marks

Exclamation marks

Some sentences are said with lots of emotion. These are called **exclamations**.
EXAMPLE: Oh no!

When we write something down as an exclamation we can use an **exclamation mark** to show expression. Some **commands** are exclamations.
EXAMPLE: Come back here!

1 Think of a short exclamation that each of these **characters** might give. Add an exclamation mark to it.

a   b   c

2 Copy these **sentences** and replace the **full stop** with an exclamation mark where you think it is needed. The first one is done for you.
 a Come quickly. Sally has fallen and hurt her knee.
    Come quickly! Sally has fallen and hurt her knee.
 b Be quiet. The baby is asleep.
 c The traffic lights are red. Stop.
 d Oh. What a nice surprise.
 e Attention. Quick march.
 f Good boy. I am very pleased with you.

Glossary
command
character
sentence
full stop

3 Draw pictures showing each of these exclamations being used.
 a Look out!   **b** Fire!   **c** Danger!

56

Diagrams

UNIT·4 **Writing to instruct**

Reading skills: *pictorial information*

Sometimes **instructions** are given in the form of pictures, diagrams and signs.

EXAMPLE: This sign instructs us not to smoke.

1. What do these signs tell us to do?

   a   b   c

Remember
The words in a title start with **capital letters**.

2. The diagrams below tell us how to do something. Write a **title** for the diagrams which says what the goal is.

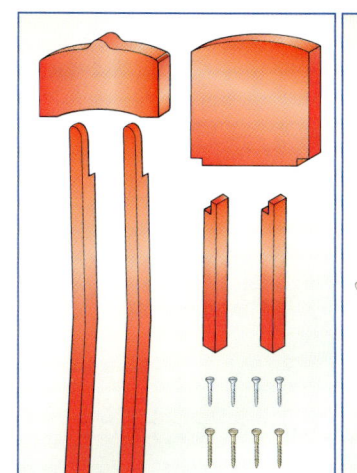

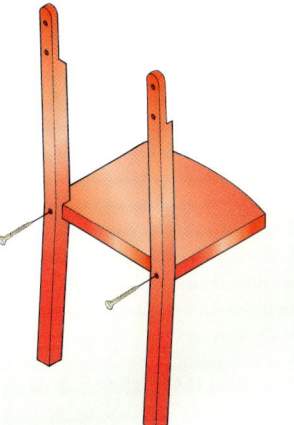

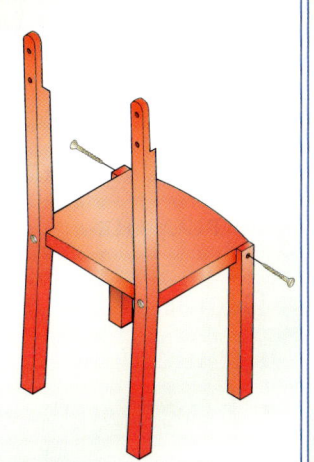

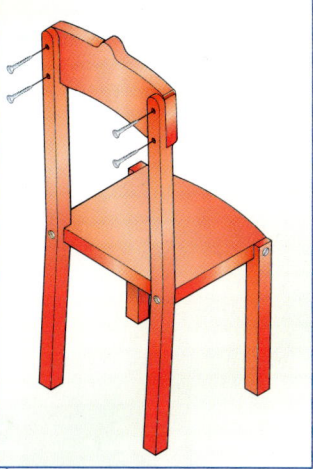

3. Look at the diagrams above and make a **list** of what parts you will need to follow the instructions.

Parts List

two front legs
two back legs

4. An **account** of how the chair was made is given below. Rewrite the passage as a set of numbered instructions which go with the diagrams above. The first one is done for you.

> First I got out all the pieces and checked they were there. Next I attached the seat to the back legs with screws. Then I attached the two front legs with screws. Finally I put the back of the chair on with screws.

1 First get out all the pieces and check they are there.
2

Glossary
instructions
capital letter
title
list
account

57

Writing instructions

You have looked at writing instructions in this unit. Now you are going to write your own instructions about how to make something or how to do something.

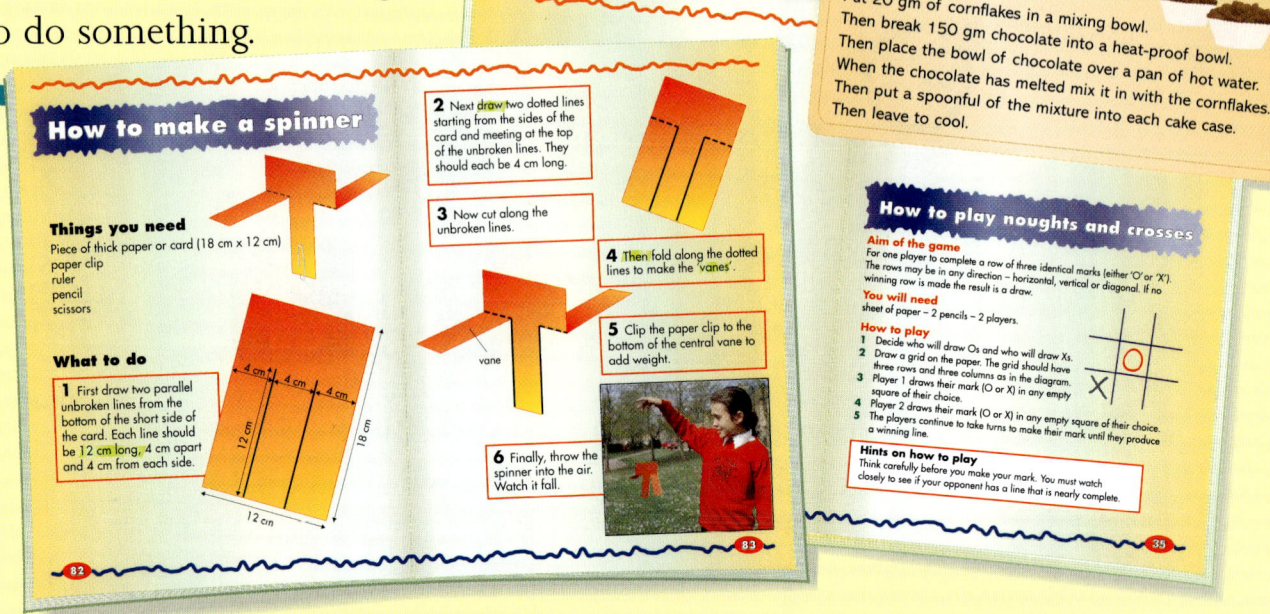

1 Reread 'How to make a spinner' (page 46), 'How to play noughts and crosses' (page 54), and any other instructions.

2 Decide what instructions you are going to write. It could be:
- how to make something, e.g. a toy, puppet or book
- how to cook something, e.g. a cake or favourite meal
- how to get somewhere, e.g. from home to school
- how to look after something, e.g. a pet or bike.

Brainstorm

3 Brainstorm the things you will need to include.

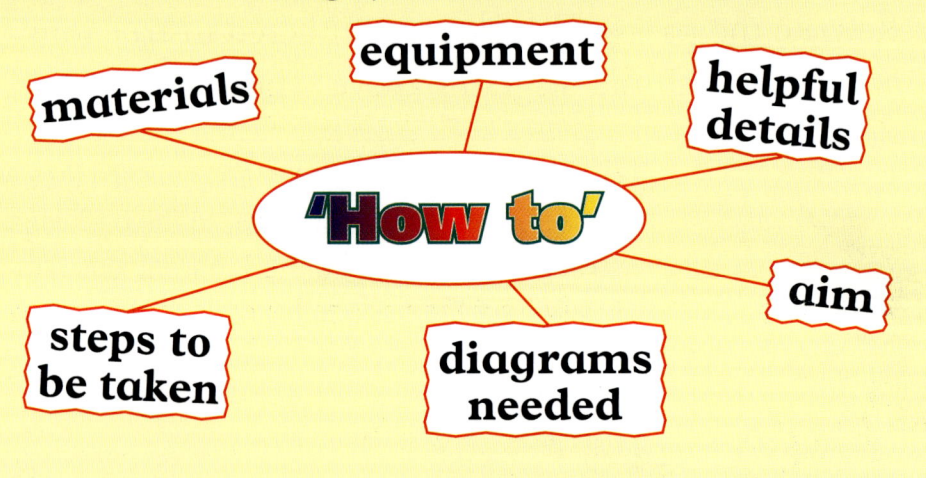

- materials
- equipment
- helpful details
- aim
- diagrams needed
- steps to be taken

'How to'

4 Make detailed notes under each heading of your brainstorm.

5 Now write a first draft starting with 'How to make …'. Use headings to help you.

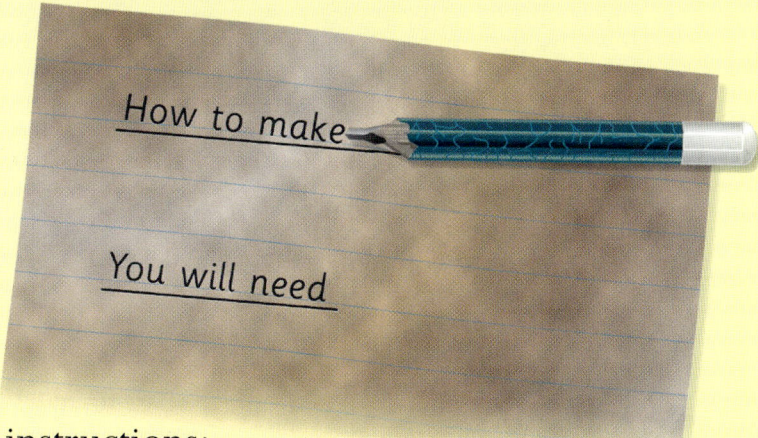

How to make

You will need

6 Check your instructions:
- have imperative verbs
- have a title which explains the goal
- are in the correct order
- have adverbs for detail
- have diagrams if needed.

7 Swap your first draft with a partner. Ask them to see if they understand exactly what they have to do. Get them to say if any of the instructions are not clear.

8 Make any alterations that will improve your instructions.

9 Write your final version.

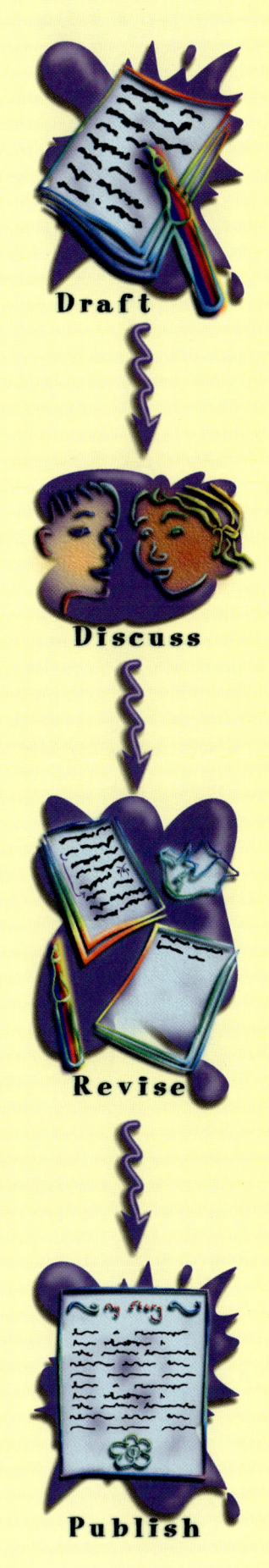

Draft

Discuss

Revise

Publish

UNIT·5
Writing to recount

In this unit you will study how letters and postcards are written. You will look at how writers tell other people what they have done and thought. At the end of the unit you will write about something you have done.

greeting
introduction
events
conclusion
closure

Dear Grandma and Grandpa,

We are at Disneyland in California. We arrived yesterday. At the hotel I had a swim in the pool until bedtime. Today I went on the rides and then I had real hot dogs.

I am having a lovely time.

Love Lizzie

Mr and Mrs King
72 Morpeth Road
GLASGOW
G37 5RZ
Scotland
UK

UNIT·5 Writing to recount

Text study: recount introduction, events, conclusion

- Why were these postcards written? Who to?
- When did the events take place? How do you know?
- Who wrote the postcards?
- What did the writer feel like when she wrote the cards?
- What events mentioned on the postcards are the same?
- What is different about the way the postcards are written?

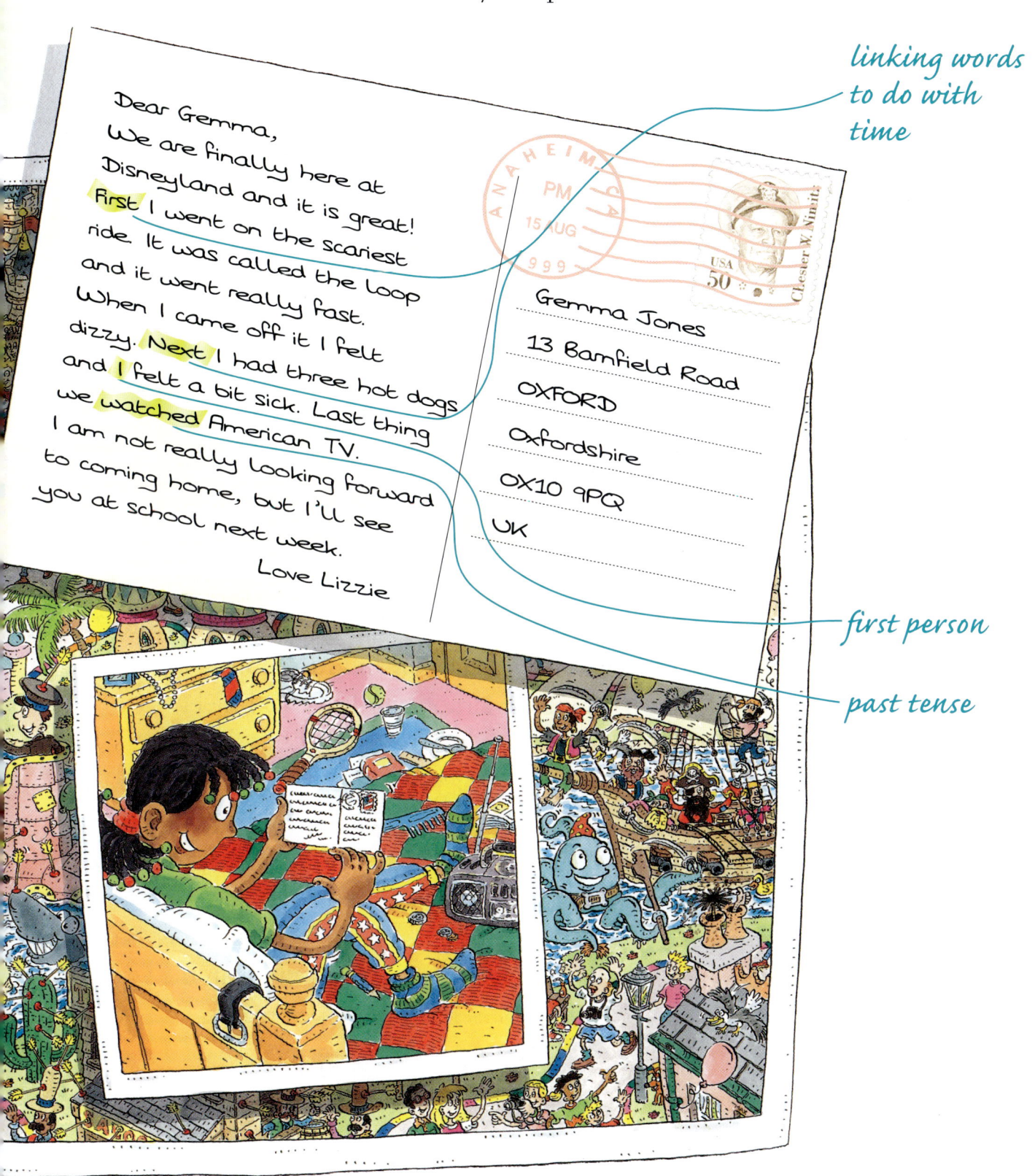

Dear Gemma,
We are finally here at Disneyland and it is great! First I went on the scariest ride. It was called the Loop and it went really fast. When I came off it I felt dizzy. Next I had three hot dogs and I felt a bit sick. Last thing we watched American TV. I am not really looking forward to coming home, but I'll see you at school next week.
   Love Lizzie

Gemma Jones
13 Barnfield Road
OXFORD
Oxfordshire
OX10 9PQ
UK

linking words to do with time

first person

past tense

61

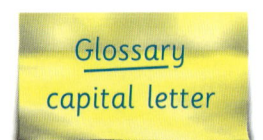

UNIT·5 Writing to recount

Reading skills: comprehension
Vocabulary: dates

Informing others

22 August 1998

Dear Simon,
I am having a great time here. It is totally different from home. First of all I joined the kids' club where I played all the games and met a friend called Brad. Next we watched the windsurfers, then we had a lesson in windsurfing. Finally I got the hang of it, but I fell over a lot. I am looking forward to another action-packed day tomorrow. See you next week.
Love Rhys

Simon Evans
6 Ladysmith Road
Penylan
CARDIFF
CF2 5PQ
Wales
UK

1 Read the postcard carefully and answer the questions.
   a The postcard was written by
      Rhys?   Simon?   Simon's mum?
   b The postcard was sent from
      a mountain village?   the seaside?   a city?
   c The postcard was sent to
      Rhys?   Simon?   the whole class?
   d List three things Rhys has done on holiday.
   e How do you think the writer of the postcard is feeling?
   f How old do you think Simon and Rhys might be?
   g Where do you think Simon and Rhys will meet the following week?

month (August – 8th month)
day of the month **22 8 98** *last two digits in the year*
(22nd August) *(nineteen ninety-eight – 1998)*

2 Dates on postmarks are written as numbers. The first number is the day of the month. The second number is the month. The last number is the final two digits in the year. Write out in full the dates from these postmarks.

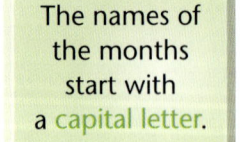

   a ABINGDON OXON 17.8.99
   b CANNON STREET BRISTOL 25.10.98
   c SOUTHHAMPTON 11.09.98
   d CARDIFF 06.01.99

Remember
The names of the months start with a capital letter.

Glossary
capital letter

UNIT·5 Writing to recount

Grammar: verb tense

Past and present

The **tense** of a **verb** tells us when something is happening: now, in the past or in the future.

This is what Joe is doing and feeling now. This is the present tense.

The postcard also says what Joe did yesterday. This is the past tense.

> 11/07/98
> Dear Sam,
> I am in Blackpool. I am enjoying the sun and playing on the beach. Yesterday evening I saw the lights, went on a tram and climbed up the tower. I wish you were here.
> Love Joe

1 Here is a **list** of verbs in the present tense. Write down the past tense of these verbs.

   Present tense: see
                         pick
                         think
                         hope
                         do

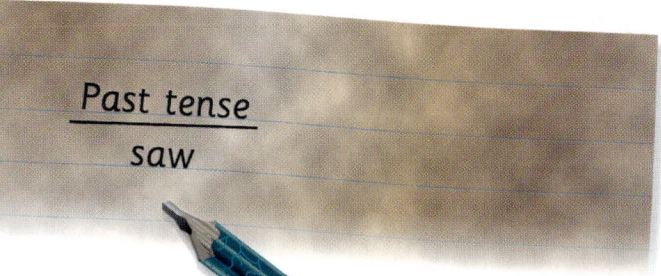

   Past tense
   saw

2 Write a **sentence** containing each of the verbs in the past tense.

   EXAMPLE: I saw three ships go sailing by.

3 The sentences in the chart are in the present tense. Write them out, changing the verb so that they are in the past tense. The first has been done for you.

Happening now – the present	Already happened – the past
The baby is crying.	The baby cried.
The little boy is skipping.	
He is feeling sad.	
My cat is jumping off the wall.	
Harry is reading a good book.	

Glossary
verb
list
sentence

UNIT·5 Writing to recount

Grammar: verb tense

Forming the past tense

Many **verbs** form the past **tense** by adding -ed. They are called **regular verbs**. Verbs that do not have -ed in the past tense are called **irregular verbs**.

1. Here is a **list** of verbs in the present tense. Write down the past tense of these verbs.

    Present tense: jump
    kick
    graze
    punch
    pick

    Past tense
    jumped

    These verbs are regular. They end in -ed in the past tense.

2. Write down the past tense of these irregular verbs

    Present tense: think
    run
    feel
    read
    write

    Past tense
    thought

    You can look up the past tense of a verb in the dictionary.

    the part of speech
    headword
    the present tense
    the past tense
    example

    a b c d e f **g** h i j k l m n o p

    guess *verb* **guesses, guessing, guessed**
    to say what you think the answer is when you do not really know.
    Did you guess the right answer?
    guest *noun* **guests**

    Glossary
    verb
    tense
    list

3. Copy the chart and use the dictionary to fill in the blanks.

Present tense	Past tense	Dictionary page
guess, guesses, guessing	guessed	90
come		
inform		
swim		

64

UNIT·5 Writing to recount
Grammar: *pronouns*

He, she, it, they

Pronouns are words which stand in the place of a **noun**.

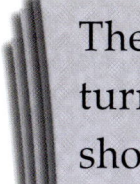

The boy walked along the street and then the boy turned the corner. The boy went past the sweet shop and then the boy went into the toy shop.

1 Read this passage to yourself. It sounds strange because the word 'boy' has been used too often. Instead of 'the boy' we could write 'he' sometimes. The word 'he' is a pronoun. Write out the passage above, replacing the words highlighted with the pronoun 'he'.

Personal pronouns take the place of the names of other people (**you**, **he**, **she**, **they**), ourselves (**I**, **we**), animals (**he**, **she**, **it**, **they**) and things (**it**, **they**).

2 Write out the **sentences** below, replacing the words highlighted with a pronoun (he, she, it, they).
   a Sally ran so fast that Sally fell over.
   b Dad was cross because Dad had dented the car.
   c The car was in the garage because the car was dented.

3 Write out the pronouns (he, she, it or they) which can go in place of the words underlined in these sentences.
   a Lunch was great. Lunch was burger and chips.
   b The whole class came to my party. The whole class really enjoyed it.
   c Justine is on holiday. Justine is in Florida.
   d George wears glasses. George needs them to see.

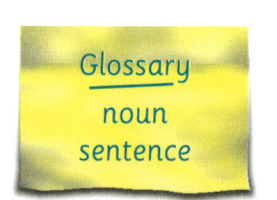

Glossary
noun
sentence

65

UNIT·5 Writing to recount

Grammar: first person pronoun

Me, myself, I

We write in the **first person** using 'I', 'me' and 'myself' to tell others about our thoughts or actions.
EXAMPLE: **I** fell in the river.
The first person is used for letters, diaries and autobiographies.

1. Rewrite the **sentences**, using the first person, as if the **events** had happened to you.
   EXAMPLE: He burnt his hand on the cooker.
   I burnt my hand on the cooker.
   a. She was too scared to go on the rollercoaster.
   b. Although it was sunny, he felt cold.
   c. He jumped on the bicycle and rode off.
   d. She dived into the swimming pool.

2. Read this **account** of Ben's breaktime.

Ben was dying to have a go on Simon's new roller skates, even though roller skates were not allowed in the playground. He made sure the teacher wasn't looking and put on his skates. Then he got up and held on to the wall. First he took a few shaky steps. Then he started rolling so fast he couldn't stop. Ben crashed into a pile of milk crates. He broke all the bottles and got soaked.

Glossary
sentence
event
account

3. Rewrite the account as if you were Ben writing in his diary. Start with today's date and 'I ...'.

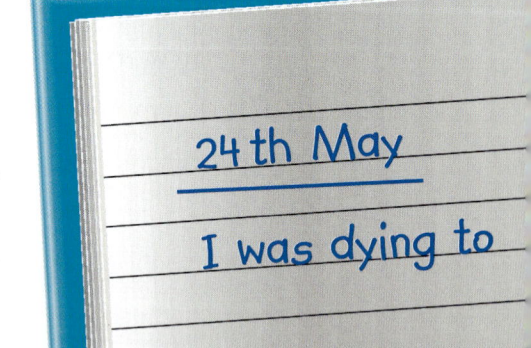

24th May

I was dying to

Time lines

UNIT·5 Writing to recount

Text study: chronological order
Grammar: chronological connectives

The order in which **events** happened is called **chronological order**. In postcards, letters and diaries the events are often written in chronological order.

Here is Ben's time line for the day he broke the milk bottles.

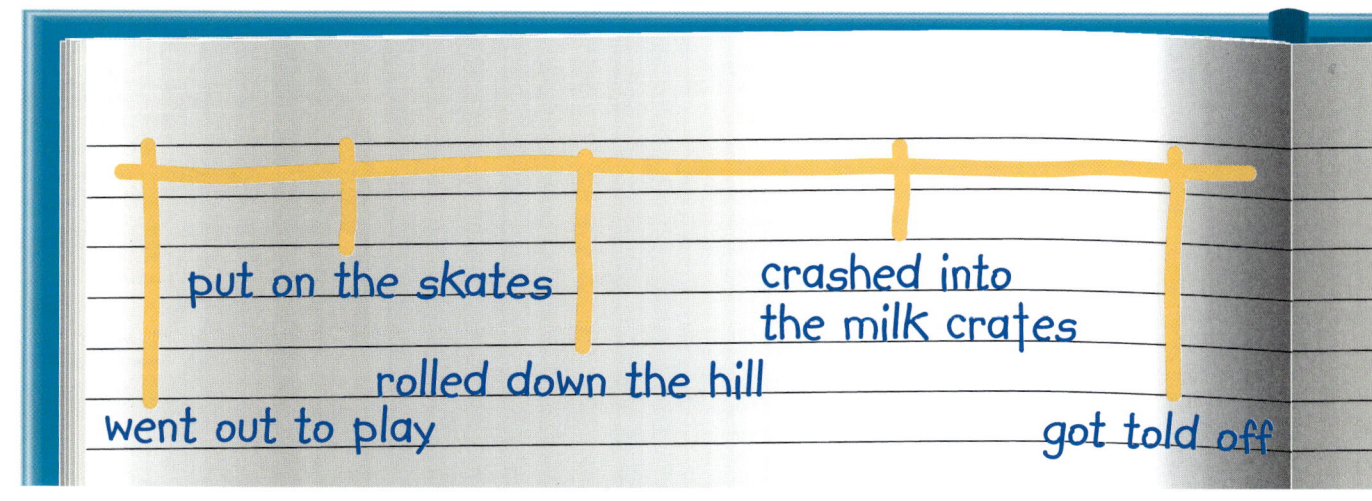

- put on the skates
- crashed into the milk crates
- rolled down the hill
- went out to play
- got told off

1 Make a time line like Ben's to show the order of the events when Gita went on a school trip to the museum.

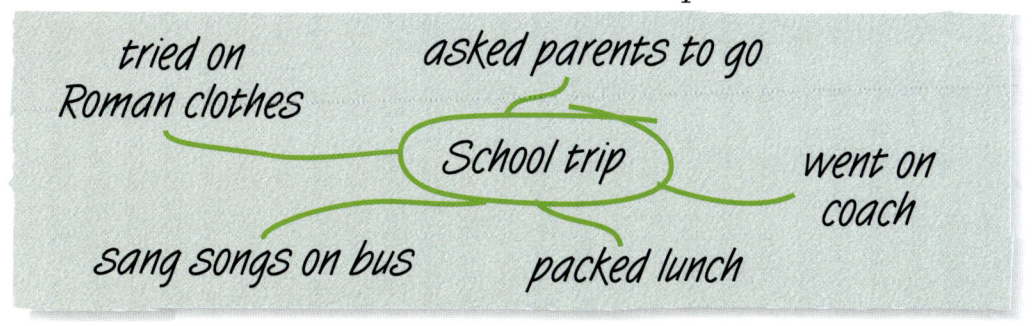

- tried on Roman clothes
- asked parents to go
- School trip
- went on coach
- sang songs on bus
- packed lunch

To write an account in chronological order we use time words to link events. These are called **connectives**: **then**, **next**, **afterwards**, **finally**.

2 Write five full **sentences**, one for each of the events in Gita's trip. Use the connectives: first, then, finally, now, next, afterwards.

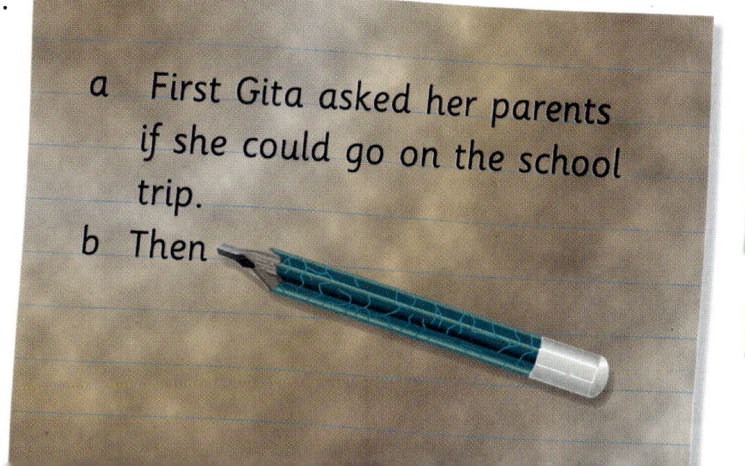

a First Gita asked her parents if she could go on the school trip.
b Then

Glossary
event
sentence

Two types of letter

You have looked at how postcards are written.
Now look at how letters are written.

13 Park Road
PONTYPRIDD
Wales
P13 4NY
13 March 1999

Dear Alex,

Today I got into trouble at school so I'm writing to tell you about it.

I met Simon Hughes who got a great new pair of skates for his birthday. At breaktime he said I could have a go on them. First I put on the skates. I held on to the wall very carefully to get started. Then I forgot that the playground was on a hill and I let go of the wall. I went faster and faster and finally I crashed into some crates full of milk bottles. The noise was amazing and I broke about twenty bottles of milk.

I've got to write a letter to the Head to tell her what happened. Do you think it is all my fault? What should I say?

Love from
Ben

---

13 Park Road
PONTYPRIDD
Wales
P13 4NY

14 March 1999

Dear Mrs Jones,

I am writing to tell you what happened in the playground.

Yesterday I forgot that we were not allowed to use skates at school. I tried out Simon Hughes' roller skates in the playground. Then I lost control and rolled down the hill. I bumped into the milk crates and broke some bottles. Mr Hawkins was very cross with me and told me to write to you.

I am very sorry for what happened.

Yours sincerely

B. Smith

Ben Smith

UNIT·5 Writing to recount

Writing skills: letter layout
Text features: formal and informal language

1 Answer each of these questions with a **sentence**.
   a Where did the accident happen?
   b Who did the skates belong to?
   c Who is the headteacher of Ben's school?
   d Which teacher told Ben off?
   e What was the school rule about roller skates?
   f Who do you think Alex is?

2 Copy out two sentences containing **verbs** in the present **tense** from the letters.
   EXAMPLE: *I am very sorry.*

Remember
Present tense says what is happening now.

Both these letters are about the same events but they are different because they are written to different people.

3 Make a list of the ways the letters sound different. What makes the first letter **informal**? What makes the second letter **formal**?

> Most letters start with a **greeting** like *Dear...* . Then the person's first name or second name, depending on how formal the letter is. At the end of the letter there is a **closure** like *Love from* or *Yours sincerely*.

4 Complete the chart.

Dear Grandad,
Love Amy
Dear Mr Jefferies,
Dear Miss Smith,
Best wishes Amy Price
Love Fred
Dear Sally,
Yours sincerely J Nagib Mr J Nagib

Glossary
sentence
verb
tense
informal language
formal language

Subject of the letter	Greeting	Closure
A letter from Amy to her good friend Sally.		
A letter to Miss Smith, Amy's teacher, from Amy Price.		
A letter to Mr Jefferies, a businessman, from Mr Nagib. The two men have never met.		
A letter from Fred to his grandfather.		

69

UNIT·5 Writing to recount

Text study: addresses

Addresses

We write addresses on envelopes and at the top of letters.

Miss J Wood
16 Elsinore Road
CHELMSFORD
Essex
CM2 9QR

35 Windmill Rise,
Southampton,
SO2 7RX

10 April 1999

1 Answer the questions in **sentences**.
   a Why do we write addresses on envelopes?
   b Why do we write addresses at the top of letters?
   c Why is the town name in **capital letters**?
   d Why is it important to write addresses clearly?
   e Why do we write a postcode?

2 Write out your address clearly.

3 Make up an address for these **characters**.

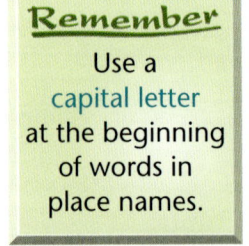

Remember
Use a capital letter at the beginning of words in place names.

Goldilocks

Batman

Wicked Witch

Glossary
sentence
capital letter
character

Include a house number; a street name; the name of a town, city or village; a county and a postcode.

70

Questions and statements

A **statement** is a **sentence** which gives us information.
A **question** is a type of sentence used when we want to know something.

I hope you are well.
When are you coming to visit me?
Love
Julie

— statement
— question

I am having a great time. What is your holiday like?
Love Gemma

— question mark

Questions end with a **question mark**.

UNIT·5 Writing to recount
Text study: questions
Punctuation: question marks

1 Write out these sentences adding question marks and **capital letters**.
   a why did you put on the skates
   b where have you been on holiday
   c whose hat is this
   d what is in the box

Questions often use these words:

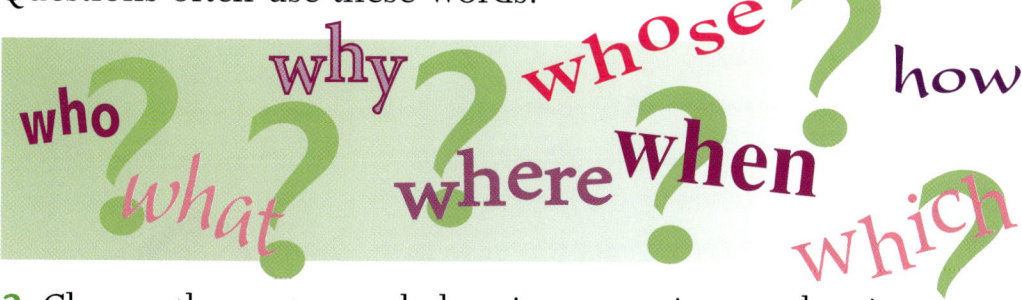

who what why whose how where when which

2 Change the sentences below into questions and write them out. Use one of the question words in each question. The first one has been done for you.
   a Here is the computer.   *Where is the computer?*
   b He put the sweets into a paper bag.
   c We are going swimming.
   d Her cat is called Flossie.

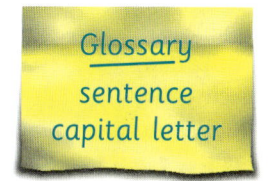

Glossary
sentence
capital letter

71

Writing a letter

You have looked at postcards and letters in this unit. Now you are going to plan and write a letter to inform someone about events in your life.

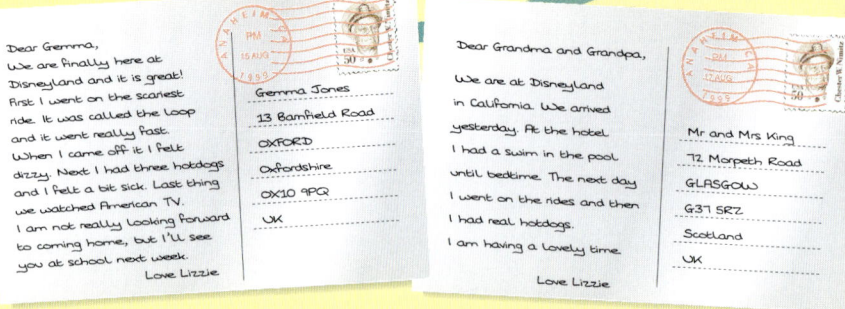

1. Look at the postcards and letters on pages 60, 61 and 68.

2. Decide who you are going to write to and what you are going to write about. The chart below might give you some ideas.

Audience for the letter	Subject of the letter	Tone of language	Closure
a penfriend	information about yourself	friendly and informal	Best wishes
a friend at school	information about a recent trip or event at school	informal	Love
your teacher	information about your home or family	friendly but formal	Yours sincerely

3. Think of questions the person you are writing to might ask.

When did you go?
Where did you go?
What was there?
Who went with you?

4. Brainstorm the content of your letter by making a web of the events you wish to include.

Brainstorm

UNIT·5 Writing to recount

5 Make a time line of the events so that they are in the right order.

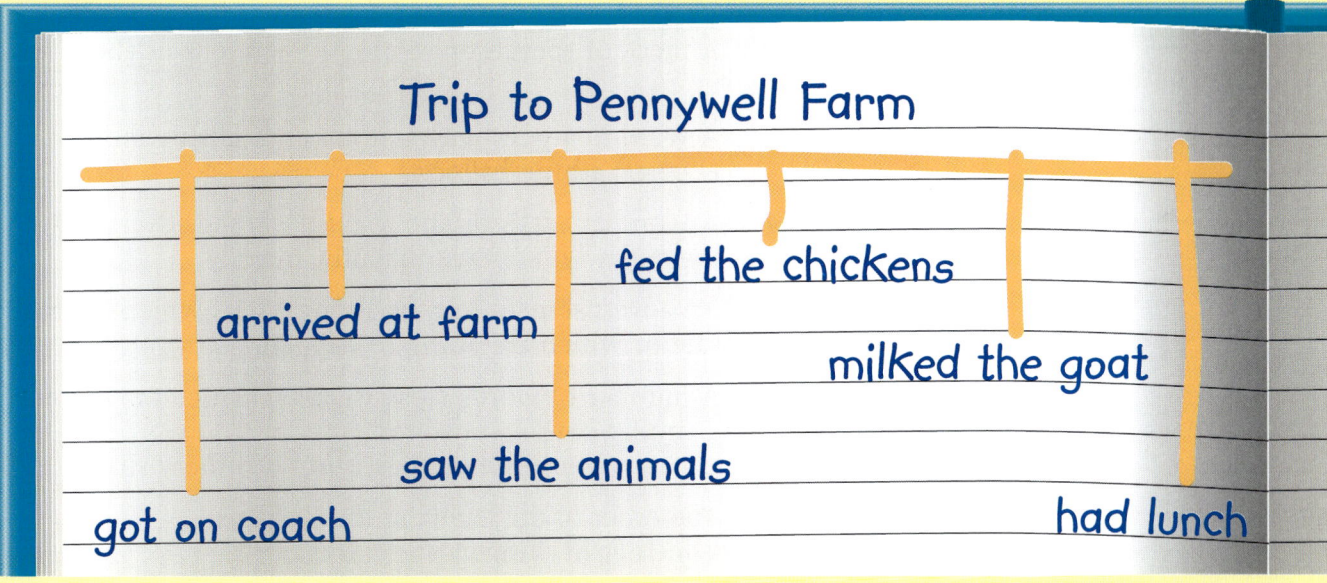

Trip to Pennywell Farm

- got on coach
- arrived at farm
- saw the animals
- fed the chickens
- milked the goat
- had lunch

6 Choose your greeting and closure. How well do you know the person you are writing to? How formal or informal will you be?

7 Write a draft of your letter. Start with an introduction and end with a conclusion.

8 Discuss your draft with a friend. Mark any changes on the draft.

we got there. We went round ~~seeing~~ *looking at* the animals. There are enormous pigs, some sheep, ~~calfs~~ *calves* and a shire horse. ~~I milked~~ *got the chance to milk* the goat. I fed the chickens.

Draft

Revise

Publish

9 Write out your letter, making sure you have written your address carefully at the top.

73

Glossary

account	A piece of speech or writing which tells us about an event.
adjective	A word that goes with a noun and tells us about it. EXAMPLE: a **blue** balloon
adverb	A word that tells us about a verb. Some adverbs have the suffix **ly**. EXAMPLES: happily, merrily
advertisement	An advertisement tells us about things which are for sale or which are going to happen.
alliteration	A number of words close together which begin with a similar consonant sound. EXAMPLES: **t**en **t**ired **t**eddies, **s**liding **s**lithery **s**nakes
alphabetical order	The order of the letters in the alphabet: a b c d e f g h i j k l m n o p q r s t u v w x y z. Word, phrases or sentences can be put in alphabetical order by putting the beginning letters in order.
antonym	An antonym is a word with the **opposite** meaning to another word. EXAMPLES: hot-cold, old-new
apostrophe	An apostrophe is a mark used to show that a letter has been left out. EXAMPLE: he is can be written as he's
argument	A written argument makes a point and gives evidence to support it.
author	A person who writes books, stories, poems etc.
blurb	A piece of writing that tells you about the content of a book. It is often on the outside back cover or inside the front cover.
brainstorm	A way of writing down ideas when planning writing. Words are arranged around the topic you are thinking about.
bullet point	A bullet point is a punctuation mark used to emphasize items in a list. EXAMPLE: • sugar • milk
capital letter	The capital letters are: A B C D E F G H I J K L M N O P Q R S T U V W X Y Z.
category word	A category word describes a set of items. EXAMPLE: the category word **footwear** includes shoes, slippers, socks etc.
character	A character is an individual in a story, play or poem. The things they do and say tell us what they are like.
chronological order/non-chronological	Chronological order is the order in which events happen. Chronological writing is written in time order. EXAMPLE: an account of a day that starts in the morning and goes through to the evening. Non-chronological writing is not written in time order.

closure	The words used before the writer's signature at the end of a letter. EXAMPLES: Love from..., Yours sincerely, or Yours faithfully.
comma	A punctuation mark used to break up sentences so that they are easier to understand. Commas are used to separate items in a list that is part of a sentence. EXAMPLE: I bought eggs**,** fish and some chocolate.
command	A sentence telling someone to do something. One of four sentence types (exclamation, question and statement are the others).
compound word	A word made from two other words. EXAMPLE: footpath
conclusion	The ending of a piece of speech or writing.
conjunction	A conjunction is a word used to join sentences or parts of sentences. EXAMPLES: and, but, then, because
connective	A word or group of words which links sentences or parts of sentences. EXAMPLES: and, then, but, even, so
consonant/ vowel	In the English alphabet there are 5 vowels (a e i o u) and 21 consonants (b c d f g h j k l m n p q r s t v w x y z).
definition	A statement giving the meaning of a word or phrase.
description	Words which enable the reader/listener to form an idea of an object, event or feeling.
dictionary entry	Information given about a word in a dictionary.
draft	A piece of writing which is not in finished form. A final draft is a piece of writing that is finished.
edit	To change the grammar, spelling, punctuation or words in writing before it is finished.
event	Something which happens.
exclamation	A type of sentence that expresses strong feeling. Exclamations end with an exclamation mark. EXAMPLE: Help me, please**!** One of four sentence types (question, statement and command are the others).
exclamation mark	A punctuation mark used at the end of a sentence to indicate strong feelings. EXAMPLE: Help**!**
fiction/non-fiction	Fiction is an invented story, poem or play. Non-fiction is writing about real events, feelings or things.
first person	The first person pronoun is I. In writing it is used when the writer is writing about him or herself.
formal language/ informal language	Formal language is the speech and writing we use for people we do not know well. EXAMPLE: How do you do? Informal language is the language we use to people we know well. EXAMPLE: Hi!

75

full stop	A full stop is a mark used to end a sentence when the sentence is not a question or exclamation. EXAMPLE: The cat sat on the mat**.**
gender words (masculine and feminine)	Gender words tell you about the sex of the person or animal. They can only apply to either men or women, not both. EXAMPLE: prince (masculine gender) and princess (feminine gender)
greeting	The words used to begin a letter. Usually **Dear…**
homonym	Words with the same form but different meanings. EXAMPLES: Lucy **saw** a lion. Tom uses a **saw** to cut wood.
homophone	Words with the same sound but different meanings. EXAMPLE: **reed** and **read**
illustration	A picture, plan or diagram which is part of a text.
imperative	An imperative sentence commands or tells the reader or listener to do something. EXAMPLE: Run over there.
instructions	Instructions tell us how to do something.
introduction	The beginning of a piece of writing.
label	The words which tell us about part of a diagram, picture or map.
language	Language is what people use to share their thoughts with each other. We talk with our voices. This is spoken language. When we write we use written language.
list	A group of things or names written down one after the other.
noun	A word that names a person, feeling, thing or idea.
onomatopoeia	Words which sound like their meaning. EXAMPLES: bang, crash
persuade	To persuade is to try to make or convince someone to believe or do something.
plan	To work out what to say or write. Notes used to start a piece of writing.
plot	The plan or main facts of a story.
plural	More than one.
poem	A piece of writing which uses words and word order to create images and ideas. The lines often rhyme.
poet	A person who writes poems.
preposition	A word telling us about the place of nouns or pronouns. EXAMPLES: on, under, in
pronoun/ personal pronoun	Pronouns are words which stand in the place of a noun. Personal pronouns take the place of the names of people.

proper noun	Words that name particular people, things or feelings. Proper nouns begin with capital letters. EXAMPLES: Christmas, London, Jamilla
punctuation	A way of marking writing using full stops, capital letters, question marks etc. This helps the reader to understand.
question	A sentence which needs a response. It ends with a question mark. EXAMPLE: What is your name? One of four sentence types (exclamation, statement and command are the others).
question mark	The punctuation mark at the end of a sentence.
regular/ irregular verb	Verbs which form the past tense by adding -ed are regular. Others do not add -ed. They are irregular verbs.
revise	To make changes to a piece of writing to improve it.
rhyme	Words which have the same ending sounds. EXAMPLES: man, pan
rhythm	The 'beats' in a piece of writing when it is read aloud or spoken
sentence	A sentence is a piece of language that can stand by itself and makes sense. There are four sentence types: exclamation, question, statement and command.
setting	The time and place of events in a story.
simile	A sentence or group of words which compares something to something else. EXAMPLE: As free as a bird.
singular	One of something.
speech marks	The inverted commas that go around what is actually said in direct speech. EXAMPLE: "I want my teddy," said the little boy.
statement	A type of sentence which tells us something. EXAMPLE: I am called Jane. One of four sentence types (question, exclamation and command are the others).
tense, past tense, present tense	Tense tells us when something is happening. Past tense: something has already happened. EXAMPLE: I **sat** down. I **was sitting** down. Present tense: something is happening now. EXAMPLE: She **is sitting** down. She **sits** down. Future tense: something which will happen. EXAMPLE: She **will sit** down
title	The heading which tells us what writing is about.
verb	A verb is a word that tells us what people are doing or being. EXAMPLE: The girls **ran** away.
verse	A part of a poem.
vocabulary	Our vocabulary is the words we know and use.

	Genre focus	Range of texts	Text features	Reading skills
UNIT 1	Writing to inform: non-chronological report	non-chronological report information texts about the skeleton and the teeth charts fiction and non-fiction extracts lists use of dictionary	opening definition logically-ordered paragraphs diagrams fiction and non-fiction charts	literal and inferential comprehension questions extracting information from charts evaluating information
UNIT 2	Writing to entertain: story	story beginnings descriptions charts dialogue	narrative openings setting plot blurbs chronological order direct speech dialogue descriptions	literal and inferential comprehension questions chart completion selecting information/ events from a text
UNIT 3	Writing to express: poetry	list poems descriptions	similes rhyme alliteration imagery	literal and inferential comprehension questions chart completion
UNIT 4	Writing to instruct: instruction	recipe diagrams story dictionary pages	lists imperative sentences (commands) chronological order technical terms	literal and inferential comprehension questions using a dictionary interpreting pictorial information sequencing passages
UNIT 5	Writing to recount: chronological recount	postcards postmarks letters addresses timelines charts lists dictionary entries	chronological connectives dates in writing and figures formal and informal language orientation events reorientation addresses greetings closures letter layout	literal and inferential comprehension questions using dictionaries reading from charts

Writing skills	Grammar	Punctuation	Words
writing sentences reading sentences completing a chart brainstorming planning a report drafting a report revising a report	sentences verbs in sentences verb 'to be' past and present tense	commas in lists	labels technical words homonyms gender nouns
writing sentences reading sentences brainstorming making a flow diagram of events drafting a story revising a story	common nouns in sentences proper nouns for names adjectives in sentences	speech marks	word meanings recognizing common nouns proper nouns for names
writing sentences reading sentences brainstorming ideas planning a poem drafting a poem revising a poem	verbs prepositions conjunctions singular and plural nouns in sentences	commas in lists	rhyming words antonyms category words compound words singular and plural nouns (inflexion)
writing sentences reading sentences planning instructions brainstorming drafting instructions revising instructions	exclamations adverbs of manner connectives chronological connectives imperative verbs	exclamation marks	abbreviations alphabetical order definitions
writing sentences reading sentences planning letters questioning brainstorming plotting time lines drafting a letter drafting an account of events editing a letter	verb tense pronouns regular and irregular verbs past and present tense verbs in sentences (inflection) statements questions first person pronoun	question marks and full stops	dates questioning words forming the past tense (inflection)

79

OXFORD
UNIVERSITY PRESS

Great Clarendon Street, Oxford, OX2 6DP

Oxford New York
Athens Auckland Bangkok Bogotá Buenos Aires Calcutta
Cape Town Chennai Dar es Salaam Delhi Florence Honk Kong Istanbul
Karachi Kuala Lumpur Madrid Melbourne Mexico City Mumbai
Nairobi Paris São Paolo Singapore Taipei Tokyo Toronto Warsaw

and associated companies in Berlin Ibadan

Oxford is a registered trade mark of Oxford University Press

© Jane Medwell and Maureen Lewis 1999

The moral rights of the author have been asserted

First published 1999

All rights reserved. No part of this publication may be reproduced,
stored in a retrieval system, or transmitted, in any form or by any means,
without the prior permission in writing of Oxford University Press.
Within the UK, exceptions are allowed in respect of any fair dealing for the
purpose of research or private study, or criticism or review, as permitted
under the Copyright, Designs and Patents Act 1988, or in the case of
reprographic reproduction in accordance with the terms of the licences
issued by the Copyright Licensing Agency. Enquiries concerning
reproduction outside these terms and in other countries should be
sent to the Rights Department, Oxford University Press,
at the address above

This book is sold subject to the condition that it shall not, by way
of trade or otherwise, be lent, re-sold, hired out or otherwise circulated
without the publisher's prior consent in any form of binding or cover
other than that in which it is published and without a similar condition
including this condition being imposed on the subsequent purchaser

British Library Cataloguing in Publication Data
Data available

Illustrated by: Annabel Collis, Elitta Fel, Sophie Grillet, Anita Jeram,
Susan Lund, Bethan Mathews, Kevin McAleenan, Shelagh McNicholas,
Pat Moffett, Visual Image
Photographs by: The Image Bank (cover), J. Allan Cash Photo library
(p25 left), Planet Earth Pictures (p25 right), Bridgeman Art Gallery (p43),
Martin Sookias (p47 & 48)

Acknowledgements
We are grateful to the following for permission to reproduce copyright
material in this book: John Foster: for 'Shoes', © John Foster 1991, first
published in *Clothes Poems* compiled by John Foster (OUP, 1991); David Higham
Associates for Eleanor Farjeon: 'Cottage' from *The Patchwork Quilt and Other Stories*
(Longman) and 'Cats' from *The Children's Bells* (OUP); B L Kearley Ltd: for
illustration by Linda Birch in Dick King-Smith: *The Hodgeheg* (Hamish Hamilton,
1989); Oxford University Press for extracts from the *Oxford Junior Dictionary*
compiled by Rosemary Sansome, Dee Reid and Alan Spooner (1995), and the
Oxford Children's Book of Science by Professor Charles Taylor and Stephen Pople
(1994); Reed Consumer Books for extract from Jill Tomlinson:
The Owl Who Was Afraid of the Dark (Methuen Children's Books, a division of
Reed International Ltd, 1968), © Jill Tomlinson 1968; and extracts from
Janet and Allan Ahlberg: *Funnybones* (Wm Heinemann, a division of
Reed International Ltd, 1980) © Janet Ahlberg and Allan Ahlberg, 1980;
A P Watt Ltd on behalf of the author for extract from Dick King-Smith:
The Hodgeheg (Hamish Hamilton, 1989).

Despite every effort to trace copyright holders this has not been possible in
every case. If notified, the publisher will be pleased to rectify any omission or
error at the earliest opportunity.

ISBN 0 19 915550 X

Printed in Hong Kong